YOUR LIFE

5

JOHN FOSTER
KIM RICHARDSON
SIMON FOSTER

Collins

William Collins' dream of knowledge for all began with the publication of his first book in 1819. A self-educated mill worker, he not only enriched millions of lives, but also founded a flourishing publishing house. Today, staying true to this spirit, Collins books are packed with inspiration, innovation and a practical expertise. They place you at the centre of a world of possibility and give you exactly what you need to explore it.

Collins. Do more.

Published by Collins
An imprint of HarperCollins*Publishers*
77–85 Fulham Palace Road
Hammersmith
London
W6 8JB

Browse the complete Collins catalogue at
www.collinseducation.com

ISBN-13 978 0 00 719 408 7
ISBN-10 0 00 719 408 0

John Foster, Simon Foster and Kim Richardson assert their moral right to be identified as the authors of this work.

British Library Cataloguing in Publication Data. A Catalogue record for this publication is available from the British Library

Commissioned by Thomas Allain-Chapman
Managed by Abigail Woodman
Project managed by Nancy Candlin
Edited by Alyson Jones
Cover and internal design by bluepig design
Page make-up by JPD
Cover photograph: Pixland 2002/Bruno Coste
Text permissions by Jackie Newman
Photographic permissions by Thelma Gilbert
Illustrations by Tony Forbes, Nigel Jordan
Consultant reader: Jackie Reynolds, Mill Hill County High School, London
Production by Katie Butler
Printed and bound by Printing Express, Hong Kong

Acknowledgements

The Publishers gratefully acknowledge the following for permission to reproduce copyright material. Whilst every effort has been made to trace the copyright holders, in cases where this has been unsuccessful or if any have inadvertently been overlooked, the Publishers will be pleased to make the necessary arrangements at the first opportunity.

Extract from *Growing Up*, published by Merlion Publishing Company; Extract from *The Young Person's Guide to Stress*, produced by Depression Alliance. Reprinted with permission; Extract from 'Do you ever feel depressed?' from *A Young Mind's Booklet*, produced by YoungMinds © YoungMinds 2003. Used with permission; Extract from 'The lowdown on… STIs', *J17*, February 2004 pp58/59. Reprinted with permission of EMAP; *G2* 'Parents: Don't touch me there: How do you persuade teenagers there is value in virginity? – Joanna Moorhead compares US-style moral pledges with British sex education, and finds few converts' by Joanna Moorhead and Marina Cantacuzino, *The Guardian*, 12 May 2004 (c) Guardian Newspapers Limited 2004. Used by permission; 'Teenagers react against anything goes society' by Rebecca Allison, *The Guardian*, 11 March, 2004 © Guardian Newspapers Limited

2004. Used with permission; 'Avoid credit card debt, students warned', Press Association, Thursday September 18th 2003. Reprinted with permission of the Press Association; *Drugs and the law* © YouGov. Reprinted with permission; 'Human cells cloned: babies next?' by Roger Highfield and David Derbyshire, *The Telegraph*, 13 February, 2004 © Telegraph Newspapers 2004. Used with permission; 'Katie believes in God and marriage. Her mother doesn't' by Liz Lightfoot, *The Telegraph*, 11 March, 2004 © Telegraph Newspapers 2004. Reprinted with permission; 'Short skirts rule "sexist"', *The Telegraph*, 4 September, 2004 © Telegraph Newspapers 2004. Reprinted with permission; 'Ecstasy kills boy who made anti-drug film' by Sally Pook, *The Telegraph*, 7 January, 2004 © Telegraph Newspapers 2004. Reprinted with permission; 'Cannabis causes mental illness' by Sarah Womack, *The Telegraph*, 8 April 2004 © Telegraph Newspapers 2003. Reprinted with permission; 'More unsafe sex sends HIV cases soaring' by Sarah Womack, *The Telegraph*, 13 February, 2004 © Telegraph Newspapers 2004. Reprinted with permission; Extract from *Sex Ed* by Dr Miriam Stoppard, published by Dorling Kindersley 1997. Copyright © 1997 by Dorling Kindersley, text copyright © 1997 by Miriam Stoppard. Reprinted with permission; Extract from *Sexually Transmitted Diseases* by Jo Whelan, Hodder Wayland 2001. Reprinted with permission of Hodder & Stoughton Ltd; Extracts from *Tell It Like It Is* by Katie Masters published by Virgin Books Limited. Copyright © Katie Masters 2002. Reprinted with permission of Virgin Books Ltd; Extracts taken from *The First Aid Manual 8th Edition, the Authorised manual of St John Ambulance, St Andrew's Ambulance Association and The British Red Cross Society*, published by Dorling Kindersley Ltd. Reprinted with permission of the three societies and Dorling Kindersley Ltd; Extract from *First Aid* by Elizabeth Fenwick © 1980 Hennerwood Publications Ltd. Reprinted with permission of Hamlyn; Extract 'Why is homophobia damaging?' from *Homosexuality* by Rosalyn Chissick, in *The Just Seventeen Advice Book* edited by Jenny Tucker published by W H Allen in 1987. Reprinted with the kind permission of the author; Extract from *Stand Up For Yourself* by Helen Benedict, published by Hodder Children's Books 1997; 'Beat exam stress' taken from the TEENS section of the BBC website www.bbc.co.uk/teens Reprinted with the kind permission of the TEENS/BBC site; Extract from *Study Skills: a Pupil's Survival Guide* by Christine Ostler, published by Ammonite Books. Reprinted with permission; Extract 'In Your Face' from www.courses-careers.com magazine. Reprinted with permission; 'The ins and outs of part time jobs' by Carla Neeson, from http://teenzone.monster.co.uk. Reprinted with permission; Extract 'Be A Perfect Partner' from www.bbc.co.uk/radio1/onelife. Reprinted with permission of BBC/Onelife; Extract from 'Starting Work, Leaflet 1' in the moneymoneymoney series produced by the Citizenship Foundation; 'The facts behind cohabitation' from www.civitas.org.uk, reprinted with permission; 'Attitudes to marriage and cohabitation' from www.oneplusone.org.uk Reprinted with permission; 'The Wedding Planners – Think you know the facts about arranged marriages? Sunna Nasrullah sets you straight'. From www.exposure.org.uk Reprinted with permission; Extracts from 'Big Daddy' found in *Dad Magazine* issue, one page 30. Reprinted with the kind permission of Show Media; 'Parenthood' quotes taken from www.thestraighttalkingproject.co.uk Reprinted with permission; 'Being a parent' information supplied by Parentline Plus. Reprinted with their permission; 'What is a Mother?' from *Smells of Childhood* by Mary Donoghue, published by Brewin Books Ltd. Reprinted with permission; Quote by Richard, aged 19, from *Baby Fathers: New Images of Teenage Fatherhood* by Edmund Clark. Reprinted with permission.

p6, p8, p9, p11, p28, p42, p65, p80, p81, p88, p91, p93 Corbis; p46, p66, p62, p87 Getty-Images; p7, p21, p34 Reuters Picture Library; p12, p31, p39, p56, p58, p71 Rex Features; p13 Still Pictures/Jurgen Shytte; p14, p20 Associated Press; p15, p18, p38 Roger Scruton; p16, p43 Panos Pictures; p17, p32 PA/Empics; p23, p37, p50, p54 Alamy; p30 Topfoto; p33 Science Photo Library/US Dept of Energy, p36 Science Photo Library/Tim Davis, p47 Science Photo Library/Edelmann, p64 Science Photo Library/Pascal Geotgheluck; p40 EPA/Empics; p45 Solent News & Photo Agency/Simon Jones; p51, p61, p78, p84 Sally & Richard Greenhill; p63 John Walmsley/Education Photo Library; p69 Advertising Archives; p83 Bubbles Photo Library; p85 Edmund Clark.

CONTENTS

INTRODUCTION

Your Life at Key Stage 4 (14–16)

Your Life 5 and *Your Life 4* together form a comprehensive two-year course in Personal, Social and Health Education, and Citizenship at Key Stage 4. This table shows how the PSHE units and Citizenship units in the two books cover the requirements of the National Framework for PSHE and the National Curriculum Programme of Study for Citizenship.

CITIZENSHIP

Developing as a citizen

These units aim to help you to understand how you can play a full part as a citizen in British society.

YEAR 4

UNIT 1 Britain – a diverse society (Citizenship 1a, 1b, 2a, 2b, 2c)

UNIT 2 Human rights (Citizenship 1a, 2a, 2b, 2c)

UNIT 3 Rights and responsibilities (Citizenship 1a, 1h, 2a, 2b, 2c)

UNIT 4 The law of the land (Citizenship 1a, 1c, 2a, 2b, 2c)

UNIT 5 Crime and punishment (Citizenship 1a, 2a, 2b, 2c)

UNIT 6 It's your government (Citizenship 1c, 1d, 2a, 2b, 2c)

UNIT 7 It's your council (Citizenship 1d, 1f, 2a, 2b, 2c, 3b)

UNIT 8 Working for change (Citizenship 1f, 2a, 2b, 2c, 3b, 3c)

YEAR 5

UNIT 1 The UK and its relations with the rest of the world (Citizenship 1i, 2a, 2b, 2c)

UNIT 2 Human rights (Citizenship 1a, 2a, 2b, 2c)

UNIT 3 Media matters (Citizenship 1g, 2a, 2b, 2c)

UNIT 4 Business and finance (Citizenship 1e, 2a, 2b, 2c)

UNIT 5 The global economy (Citizenship 1e, 2a, 2b, 2c)

UNIT 6 Global challenges (Citizenship 1j, 2a, 2b, 2c)

UNIT 7 Environmental issues (Citizenship 1j, 2a, 2b, 2c)

UNIT 8 Working for change (Citizenship 1f, 2a, 2b, 2c, 3b, 3c)

The activities

The various activities offer you the opportunity to develop a number of important skills:

- To analyse information and to research further information from a range of sources, including the internet (Citizenship 2a)
- To share your views on topical political, social and moral issues in class discussions and debates, justifying your opinions (Citizenship 2b, 2c)
- To express your ideas in a variety of written forms (Citizenship 2b)
- To negotiate, decide and participate co-operatively in school and community projects, and to reflect on the process of participating (Citizenship 3b, 3c)

- To reflect on your personal qualities and to assess your character, achievements and potential so that you can set yourself realistic personal goals (PSHE 1a)
- To understand your emotions and how to manage them in your relationships with family and friends (PSHE 3e)
- To know how to make informed choices and how to make your own decisions (PSHE 1d)
- To take responsibility for your own health, welfare and safety (PSHE 2a)
- To recognise when unhelpful pressure is being put on you, and to use assertive techniques to combat it (PSHE 2b)

PERSONAL, SOCIAL AND HEALTH EDUCATION

Understanding yourself

This strand of the course aims to develop your confidence and responsibility.

Keeping healthy

These units are designed to help you to understand how to develop a healthy, safer lifestyle, to think about the alternatives when making decisions about personal health, and the consequences of such decisions.

Developing relationships

The aim of these units is to develop your ability to handle close relationships and to emphasise the importance of showing respect and acting responsibly in your dealings with other people.

Reviewing

This unit provides a framework for assessing the knowledge, skills and understanding developed in Citizenship, and Personal, Social and Health Education during the year.

UNIT 9 Developing your identity (PSHE 1a, 1b, 1c, 1d)

UNIT 10 Managing your emotions and moods (PSHE 1a, 1b, 1c, 1d, 3e, 3f)

UNIT 11 Thinking ahead: planning your future (PSHE 1f, 1g)

UNIT 12 Managing your money (PSHE 1e)

UNIT 13 Healthy eating (PSHE 2a, 2d)

UNIT 14 Safer sex and contraception (PSHE 2a, 2b, 2e, 2f, 3b)

UNIT 15 Drinking and smoking (PSHE 2a, 2b, 2e)

UNIT 16 Health matters (PSHE 2a, 2e, 2g)

UNIT 17 Changing relationships: friends and family (PSHE 3b, 3e, 3f 3h)

UNIT 18 Coping with crises (PSHE 3e, 3f, 3i, 3j)

UNIT 19 Challenging offensive behaviour (PSHE 3a, 3c/Citizenship 1b, 2a, 2b, 2c)

UNIT 20 Reviewing and recording your learning

UNIT 9 Developing your own values (PSHE 1b/Citizenship 2a, 2b, 2c)

UNIT 10 Managing your time and studies (PSHE 1a)

UNIT 11 Thinking ahead: planning your future (PSHE 1f, 1g)

UNIT 12 Managing your money (PSHE 1e)

UNIT 13 Managing stress and dealing with depression (PSHE 2c)

UNIT 14 Safer sex (PSHE 2a, 2b, 2e, 2f, 3b)

UNIT 15 Drugs and drugtaking (PSHE 2a, 2b, 2e)

UNIT 16 Emergency first aid (PSHE 2h)

UNIT 17 Marriage and commitment (PSHE 3e, 3g)

UNIT 18 Parenthood and parenting (PSHE 3e, 3f, 3h)

UNIT 19 Challenging offensive behaviour (PSHE 3a, 3c/Citizenship 1a, 2a, 2b, 2c)

UNIT 20 Co-operating on a community project (Citizenship 1f, 2a, 2b, 2c, 3b, 3c)

UNIT 21 Reviewing and recording your learning

1 THE UK AND ITS RELATIONS WITH THE REST OF THE WORLD

The European Union

Aim: To understand what the European Union is and how it is organised (Citizenship 1i, 2a, 2b, 2c)

What is the EU?

The EU stands for European Union. It is an international body made up of 25 different countries. The main aims of the EU are:

- To raise the quality of life for its citizens, through social development.
- To improve the economic position of its citizens, companies and countries by economic co-operation and development through economic growth.
- To promote common foreign and security policies and to create a secure environment for its citizens.

In just half a century of existence, the EU has delivered peace between its members and prosperity for its citizens. It has created a single European currency (the euro) and a borders-free 'single market' where goods, people and money move around freely.

The EU has grown from six to 25 countries, with two more due to join in 2007. It has become a major trading power.

The EU has created a borders-free single market

How does the EU work?

The EU's success owes a lot to its unique nature and the way it works, for the EU is not a group of states joined together in one country like the United States and it is not simply an organisation for co-operation between governments, like the United Nations (see page 12). The countries (member states) that make up the EU remain independent nations, but they pool their power in order to gain a strength and world influence none of them could have on their own.

The three main decision-making institutions are:

1. The European Parliament, which represents the EU's citizens and is directly elected by them.
2. The Council of the European Union, which represents the individual member states.
3. The European Commission, which seeks to uphold the interests of the Union as a whole.

This 'institutional triangle' produces the policies and laws (directives, regulations and decisions) that apply throughout the EU.

The rules and procedures that the institutions must follow are laid down in the agreements which the member states' presidents and prime ministers have accepted and have been agreed by their parliaments.

In principle, it is the European Commission that proposes new EU laws, but it is the European Parliament and the Council of the European Union that adopts them.

The European Court of Justice upholds the rule of European law, and the European Court of Auditors checks the financing of the Union's activities.

The main institutions of the EU

The European Council

- EU leaders (above) attending the European Council – a meeting of the heads of state and government of all the EU countries, plus the President of the European Commission.

- It meets four times a year to agree overall EU policy and to review progress.

- It is the highest-level policy-making body in the EU, which is why its meetings are often called 'summits'.

The European Commission

- Its job is to propose new regulations or rules for the EU and to make sure that EU laws are implemented.

- Since 2004, there has been one Commissioner nominated from each member country.

- Commissioners are meant to leave behind loyalties to their countries and act for the good of the EU. They oversee the administration of the EU, and make sure that EU regulations are enforced.

The Council of the European Union

- This is the main legislative and decision-making body of the EU.

- It consists of one minister from each member state and meets nearly 100 times a year.

- It discusses proposals put forward by the European Commission. Different ministers meet according to each different area of policy. For instance, the 25 agricultural ministers (one from each EU member state) will meet to discuss farming and fishing; the 25 finance ministers, including the UK Chancellor of the Exchequer, will meet to discuss the EU budget; and 25 foreign ministers will meet to discuss foreign affairs.

The European Parliament

- It is made up of 732 representatives, known as Members of the European Parliament, or MEPs. The UK elects 78 MEPs by proportional representation.

- Its job is to scrutinise and develop policies within the EU.

- It discusses proposals made by the European Commission and can amend them, but its decisions are not binding.

- Although it is the only directly elected body, it is the least powerful of the main institutions of the EU.

Discuss how decisions are made in the EU. Which institution do you think is the most important and holds the most power? Give reasons for your views.

❶ Discuss the aims of the EU and what it has achieved during its existence.

❷ What is unique about the EU's organisation? How is it different from the United States and the United Nations?

European elections

Elections to the European Parliament are held once every five years. But there is considerable apathy among voters and turnout is much lower than for national elections. In the 2004 European elections in the UK, the turnout was 38% compared to 59% in the 2001 general election.

Why do you think turnout for European elections is lower than for national elections?

FOR YOUR FILE

Write a letter to someone who is undecided about whether to vote in the European elections to persuade them that they ought to do so.

The UK and the EU

Aim: To explore Britain's relationship with the EU, and to discuss the issues of expansion of the EU and the euro (Citizenship 1i, 2a, 2b, 2c)

Britain and Europe

British people's attitudes towards Europe vary. Some are strongly in favour of the UK's membership in the EU and are pro-European. Many would welcome further integration, while others are less enthusiastic, hence the term 'Euro-sceptic'. While they accept the benefits of membership of the EU, they do not want to see any further powers "handed over to Brussels".

List all the ways you think the EU affects you. Share your ideas in a class discussion.

How does the EU affect us?

The EU affects our daily lives in many different ways:

- The majority of UK trade is done with other member states, so the goods we buy in our shops often come from the EU.

- Our passports are EU passports. We have the freedom to travel freely and to live and work in any of the 25 countries of the EU.

- Many areas of our lives are covered by European law, in particular such areas as business, agriculture, the environment, discrimination and civil liberties.

The expansion of the EU

A major aim of the EU has been to get as many European countries as possible to become members. Membership is open to any European state that respects 'the principles of liberty, democracy, respect for human rights and fundamental freedoms and the rule of law'.

In 1957 there were six members. In 2000 the EU had 15 members. By 2004 it had grown to 25 members. New countries that may join the EU include Romania and Bulgaria in 2007. Turkey has applied for membership, whilst other countries, such as Croatia, have expressed an interest in joining.

Supporters of EU expansion argue:	Opponents of EU expansion argue:
- that by joining the EU, democracy will continue to expand in these countries - that economic growth will accelerate, as the free trade area of the EU expands - a larger Europe will also be stronger and able to play a greater role in world affairs.	- that the EU is too big. This is because, with 25 countries involved, it has become difficult for the EU to decide anything - that as the EU increases in size, there will be a huge increase in bureaucracy.

EU institutions are also changing. One example is how the Council of the European Union is run. Previously, all countries had to agree in order for a proposal to go ahead. This was known as the national veto. However with the expansion of the EU, the number of areas that this veto applies to has shrunk. For example, there used to be a veto on fishing and now there isn't.

Some countries, such as France, want to abolish the national veto and have majority voting, where a majority of countries can decide a vote. However, countries such as the UK wish to continue with the national veto in many areas, especially that of foreign affairs.

1 Why do some people argue that the EU has grown too large? Why do others argue that expansion has been a good thing? What do you think?

2 Discuss the issue of the national veto. Do you think all decisions in the Council of the European Union should be made by a majority or are there some policy areas where the national veto should be retained? Should smaller counties have a smaller say?

Economic and monetary union

Since 1992, a key aim of the EU has been for economic and monetary union. A single currency, the euro, was created in 1999. At the time, the EU had 15 members and 12 of them decided to adopt the euro. Three countries – Denmark, Sweden, and the UK – did not adopt it.

Supporters of a single currency argue:	Opponents of a single currency argue:
• that it would eliminate exchange rates. For example, the same money can be used in Germany, France, or Italy. Usually money has to be converted to the currency of the country.	• that it would involve a loss of power. This is because the Bank of England would no longer have control of interest rates in the UK. The European Central Bank run by the EU would have control.
• that it will lead to lower costs for businesses, helping promote economic growth.	• that it would also eventually require a common taxation policy across the EU. This in turn would mean political union – the EU becoming one country, with its member states becoming regions of Europe.
• that it will bring the economies of Europe closer together. This will create greater economic stability, leading to lower interest rates in Europe, making cheaper mortgages for its citizens.	• that different parts of the European economy would grow at different speeds, meaning that some parts of Europe would lose out under the single currency.

The UK Government is committed to holding a national vote in 2006 on whether to join the single currency. The Conservative Party is against the single currency, whilst Labour and the Liberal Democrats are in favour. One smaller political party, the UK Independence Party, is in favour of leaving the EU altogether.

Design a campaign poster for the vote either for or against the single currency. Would you vote 'Yes' or vote 'No'? Think carefully about what message you want to include on your poster.

Discuss the views below. Which do you agree with and why?

"We should withdraw from Europe completely."

"Europe should become one country and the UK should just be part of that country."

FOR YOUR FILE

Write a letter to a friend explaining your views on whether Britain should be part of a single currency.

The UK and the Commonwealth

Aim: To explore the UK's relationship with the Commonwealth, and how the Commonwealth works
(Citizenship 1i, 2a, 2b, 2c)

What is the Commonwealth?

The Commonwealth of Nations (or the Commonwealth) is an international organisation made up of countries that were once part of the British Empire. It contains 54 member states, including 1.7 billion people, making up almost one-third of the world's population.

The founder member of the Commonwealth was the UK. Other major countries within the Commonwealth include Canada, Australia, New Zealand, India, and Pakistan. Many African and Caribbean countries, as well as some islands in the Pacific, are also members.

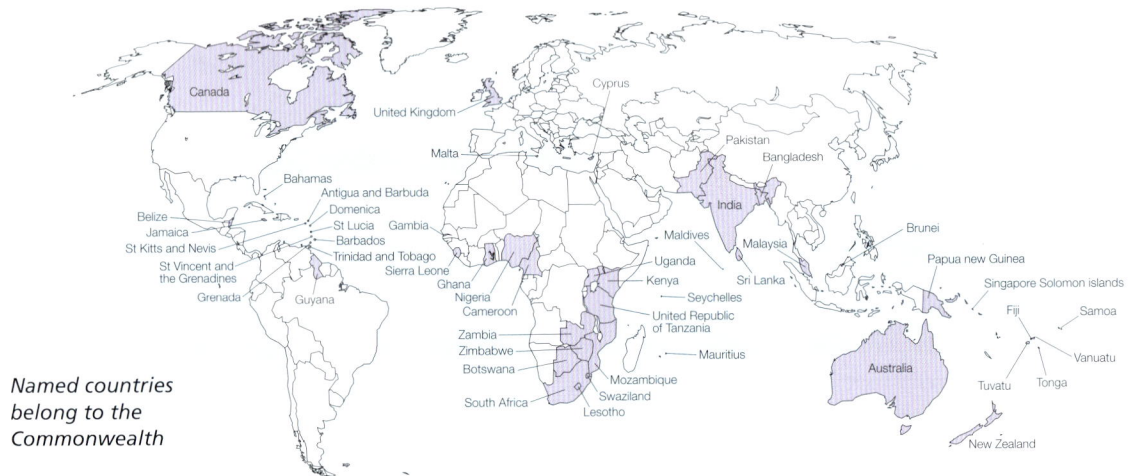

Named countries belong to the Commonwealth

The aims of the Commonwealth

The aims of the Commonwealth are similar to those of the EU (see page 6) and the UN (see page 12). Seven main aims promote the following:

1. International peace and order
2. Democracy
3. The rules of law
4. Good governance
5. Freedom of expression and human rights
6. Economic development
7. Social development

① **Discuss the different aims of the Commonwealth. Which do you think are the most important? Give reasons for your views.**

② **Draw a spider diagram showing the different aims of the Commonwealth.**

How the Commonwealth works

The Commonwealth meets formally once every two years in a member country. The British monarch, currently Queen Elizabeth II, is the Head of the Commonwealth and chairs these meetings.

The administrative headquarters of the Commonwealth is in London. The Commonwealth works to achieve its aims and to help countries in several different ways:

- By sending observers to check that elections are carried out properly, without fraud and intimidation.

- By providing training programmes for governments and companies within member countries, e.g. lawyers are sent to a less developed country to produce a report on how its legal system works.

- By sending advisers from one country to another to provide expertise and advice on economic development. For example, a group of irrigation experts are sent to an African country to train people on how to make the best use of their water supply.

- By holding conferences to discuss issues of importance to member countries. e.g. a conference is held on conflict prevention to encourage neighbouring governments to sort out their differences peacefully when they occur.

Commonwealth schemes

The Commonwealth has a number of schemes that it uses to achieve its aims. Two of these schemes are:

1. The Commonwealth Youth Credit Initiative

This is designed to promote the growth of small businesses in less developed countries. It does this by lending people small amounts of money when banks would not. These small amounts are known as 'micro-credit'.

To people in less developed countries, this is crucial as often their options will be very limited. The idea is to increase economic self sufficiency for young, poor people. This fund also provides training and long-term support to keep the businesses going.

> The scheme provides low interest rates and low training fees.

> This means that costs are kept down, which is crucial to the scheme's success.

> Money from these businesses can then be reinvested.

> This helps the businesses and the local economy to grow.

2. The Commonwealth Fund for Technical Co-operation

This fund promotes economic and social development. It does this by sending experts from one country to provide training and advice in another country. Examples include training in and agriculture, education, and legal advice.

Case study

Growing tea in Kenya

George Jabala is a tea farmer in Kenya, East Africa. The Commonwealth Fund for Technical Co-operation sent a farming adviser from Australia, who was an expert at growing crops in tropical climates. He provided George with scientific advice on how to manage when the price of tea fluctuated. He advised George to get together with other farmers to negotiate with the big tea companies. As a result, the farm now makes a profit. The extra money has been reinvested to allow the farm to expand in the future.

Discuss how the Commonwealth Fund for Technical Co-operation helped George Jabala overcome problems with his tea farm.

What difference has this made to George Jabala's business?

FOR YOUR FILE

Write a short statement explaining how the Commonwealth Youth Credit Initiative helps small businesses in less developed countries.

Enforcing the aims of the Commonwealth

If a country goes directly against the aims of the Commonwealth, it can be suspended from the organisation. If the country does not then change its behaviour, sanctions can be imposed, thus limiting trade with that country. A country that persistently breaks the rules can be thrown out of the Commonwealth. Zimbabwe was suspended from the Commonwealth due to irregularities in its elections.

❶ Discuss the statement on the right. Do you agree?

❷ Compile a table listing reasons for and against this statement.

> "Although its power and influence are ultimately limited, the Commonwealth serves a useful purpose."

The United Nations

Aim: To understand what the United Nations is, what its aims are, and to examine its role in the world (Citizenship 1i, 2a, 2b, 2c)

The United Nations

The United Nations (UN) was founded in 1945 by the countries that won the Second World War. The UK was one of the UN's founder members. Like the EU, the UN was designed to make sure that a war like the Second World War did not happen again.

The UN Charter

Around 190 countries are members of the UN. All member countries have to sign the UN Charter, which sets out the aims of the UN. These aims include:

- The development of friendly relations amongst nations.
- Co-operation on economic development.
- Co-operation on social and cultural development.
- Maintenance of international peace and security.
- Promotion of humanitarian issues that affect its member countries.

The UN General Assembly

A meeting of the UN General Assembly in 2004

The main policy-making body of the UN is the General Assembly, which meets once a year. One representative (or ambassador) from each country has the right to speak and vote. The UN General Assembly makes decisions on matters affecting the whole world, such as environmental agreements to combat global warming. However, it is not a world government and cannot tell national governments what to do.

The UN Security Council

The UN Security Council was set up to settle disputes between countries and to try to preserve world peace. The Council has five permanent members – USA, UK, France, China and Russia. There are also 10 non-permanent members, elected for a two-year period. If one permanent member disagrees on a resolution, this stops a decision (known as a 'veto'). This has often made it difficult to get resolutions passed.

The role of the UN Security Council includes:

- discussing any situation where fighting has occurred or where there is a threat to international security. Major issues discussed in 2004 were the war in Iraq and fighting terrorism.
- proposing actions and solutions, such as sanctions, political pressure or military intervention. For example, economic sanctions preventing the free trade of goods were imposed on South Africa in the late 1980s until it adopted a democratic system of government.
- taking responsibility for UN peacekeeping forces (see page 15), which are sent to areas of conflict to try to prevent more fighting and to protect civilians.

Discuss the aims of the UN and how it is organised.

The UN Secretariat

The UN Secretariat, which is based in New York, oversees the administration and running of the UN. It is headed by the Secretary-General of the United Nations. Currently this is Kofi Annan, who was elected by the General Assembly in 1997.

The many different agencies and commissions below the Secretariat deal with world problems such as hunger, poverty, injustice, ill-health and illiteracy. Examples include the UN Human Rights Commission, UN Commission for Refugees and the UN Commission for Children. The UK chooses to donate extra money to these particular commissions, as it believes these to be priority areas.

> "The UN has two decision-making chambers like the UK Parliament. True or false?"

> "The UK is a permanent member of the UN Security Council and thus has a veto. True or false?"

Draw up a quiz consisting of other true and false statements about the UN. Exchange your quiz with the pair next to you and complete their quiz.

The UN – helping to solve the world's problems

Homelessness

The UN Commission for Refugees helps people who have left their homes either as a result of wars or natural disasters. It is estimated that since the 1950s this commission has helped 50 million refugees either to return to their homeland or to start a new life elsewhere.

Environment

The UN Environment Programme aims to safeguard the global environment for future generations. As part of this, Agenda 21 was agreed at the UN summit on the environment held in Rio de Janeiro in 1992.

Health

The World Health Organisation aims to promote health throughout the world. A major focus has been immunisation programmes, which have saved millions of lives by providing protection against diseases such as measles, tetanus, tuberculosis and whooping cough.

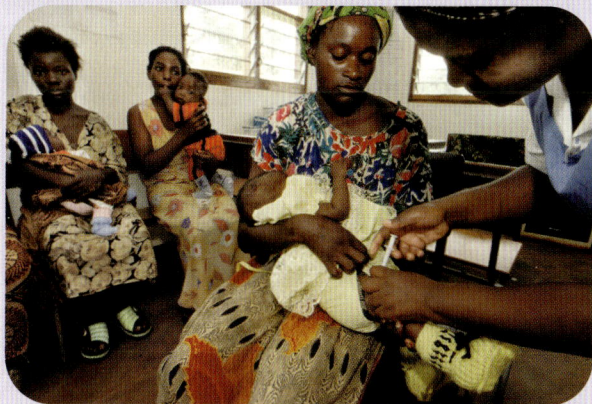

World Health Organisation immunisation programmes have helped save millions of lives

Hunger

The World Food Programme aims to fight hunger wherever it occurs, providing food to refugees and emergency relief to people suffering from famine. It also gives support to long-term development projects to ensure people can grow their own food.

FOR YOUR FILE

Draw up a list of key facts about the UN. The heading for your list is '10 things you need to know about the UN'.

Find out about two other UN bodies and the work they do. Examples could include commissions that help the economic development of poorer countries, or eradicate illiteracy.

2 HUMAN RIGHTS

Enforcing and protecting human rights

Aim: To explore human rights issues, focusing on cases of human rights abuses and looking at how human rights can be protected and enforced (Citizenship 1a, 2a, 2b, 2c)

Protecting human rights

A key way to protect human rights is to educate people. Once people know their rights, they can complain when their rights are being violated. The Universal Declaration of Human Rights argues that: "all people should be free to fulfil their potential".

Raising awareness

Raising awareness of human rights abuses is another way to protect human rights. Some pressure groups send human rights observers to conflict areas where human rights are being abused. International observers can often protect human rights, just by their very presence. For example, in the run up to the 2008 Olympic Games, human rights groups hope to use the publicity of the Olympics to pressurise the Chinese government to respect people's rights in China where there is currently religious persecution.

Prisoners at Guantanimo Bay, the US military base in Cuba

Letting governments know that human rights abuses are being noted can act as a very useful deterrent. The most successful example of this is the 'Prisoner of Conscience' Campaign run by Amnesty International. The pressure group encourages people to write to governments that are holding prisoners who have committed no real crime and whose human rights are being abused. Sometimes the prisoners are set free, sometimes not.

Pressure groups, like Human Rights Watch, also produce reports on governments each year to draw attention to their human rights record. They encourage individuals, companies and governments that respect human rights not to trade with those that don't.

Strengthening the law

Stronger laws mean greater legal protection. This is one reason why the EU has drafted the European Charter of Fundamental Rights. One of the new protections it offers is a ban on financial gain from the human body. This strengthens the law against slavery, illegal organ transplants, and the selling of surrogate babies, and it may strengthen the law against prostitution.

What do you think is the most effective way of protecting human rights? Why?

Failing to protect human rights: war crimes

Sometimes methods of protecting human rights fail. In the worst cases, governments simply ignore human rights. In Bosnia in the mid-1990s, ethnic cleansing occurred. This is when a whole ethnic group is forced to move from their homes or are killed.

Ethnic cleansing is a war crime. War crimes are large-scale human rights abuses that occur in conflicts. Another example is 'genocide', which is an attempt to wipe out a whole group of people. As a result of the Nazis attempt at genocide of the Jewish people during the Second World War, the Universal Declaration of Human Rights was established in 1948.

Enforcing human rights internationally

When protecting human rights fails, enforcement becomes necessary. This can involve prosecuting war criminals, the deployment of UN peacekeeping troops, or in extreme cases, direct military intervention and regime change.

The International Criminal Court

The International Criminal Court (ICC) was set up in 2002 and is based at The Hague in the Netherlands. The idea is it doesn't matter where the criminal committed the crime, if it was illegal under international law they will be prosecuted.

Although 60 countries have signed the treaty recognising the ICC, the USA has refused to do so. The USA says it will not have its soldiers subject to the international rules of an external court. The USA believes this would limit what they could do to intervene and protect human rights. Critics of the USA say if it wants to improve human rights around the world, it has to be subject to the same rules as everyone else.

Military intervention and regime change

Sometimes, in the case of widespread human rights abuses, only the use of force will prevent further abuses from occurring. This has led countries to use military intervention to stop human rights abuses.

The most extreme example of military intervention is regime change. This occurred in Iraq in 2003. Frustrated by years of Saddam Hussein ignoring the will of the United Nations, the USA, backed by the UK, Spain, and several other countries, invaded Iraq and overthrew Saddam Hussein's government.

UN peacekeepers

The United Nations (UN) is responsible for peacekeeping forces that are sent to areas of conflict. These soldiers come from neutral countries that are not involved in the conflict. Their job is to monitor human rights and protect them where possible, without getting drawn into the conflict. Because they are there on behalf of the UN, their presence is legal and neutral, unlike troops sent in to achieve regime change. For example, peacekeepers have successfully kept the peace in Cyprus since 1974.

UN troops keeping the peace in Cyprus

However, the use of peacekeepers in the conflict in Bosnia in the 1990s was largely judged to be a failure. In one instance, UN troops could only watch with horror as civilians were attacked and murdered only a few kilometres from the troops' position. This is because peacekeepers are not allowed to attack anyone even if that person is doing something wrong.

---

❶ Do you think that the USA was right not to join the ICC? Give reasons for your views.

> "If, in order to protect the human rights of the majority, it means violating the human rights of a few people, then that's acceptable."
> *Jonas*

> "Military intervention is fine, but regime change isn't. Everyone has the right to self-determination."
> *Mary*

❷ Look at the statements above. Do you agree or disagree with them? Why? Give reasons for your views.

Discuss the statements below. Which do you agree with? Why?

> "Peacekeepers are a waste of time. What's the point of having peacekeepers when they can't intervene to protect human rights?"
> *Karim*

> "If just one life is saved or one town protected, then UN peacekeepers are worthwhile."
> *Julie*

Human rights abuse

Aim: To explore human rights issues and to examine cases of human rights abuse (Citizenship 1a, 2a, 2b, 2c)

Basic survival needs

Basic necessities are those things that we cannot do without. These include food, clean water, shelter and clothing. These necessities are meant to be protected by Article 25 of the Universal Declaration of Human Rights, which states that:

"Everyone has the right to an adequate standard of living, including food, clothing, housing, and medical care".

Despite this, basic necessities are not met for different people across many parts of the world. For example, over 1.2 billion people out of a worldwide population of six billion do not have access to safe drinking water.

Access to basic necessities is not just a problem in less developed countries. In the UK there are almost half a million people who are homeless. Many are denied access to basic shelter, meaning that basic necessities are not being met – often right on our doorstep.

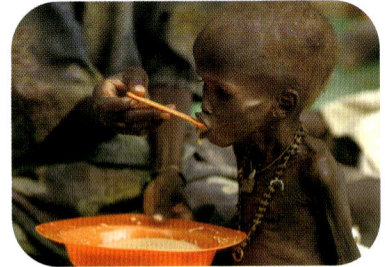

Look at the photograph. Which basic necessities do you think aren't being met?

Human rights abuses

International human rights problems are not just confined to necessities. The organisation Human Rights Watch has identified a long list of human rights abuses that occur around the world. Among the most common rights violated are the following:

Rights violated	How
● The right of self-determination	● In Zimbabwe, the result of elections held in 2002 was fixed by the Zimbabwean President, Robert Mugabe. The police and government supporters routinely attacked opponents protesting against this 'electoral rigging'. Due to the arrest of journalists that criticise the government, freedom of the press does not exist.
● The right to a fair employment	● In India, moneylenders often exploit workers by charging them high interest on loans that they can never pay back. As a result, many workers end up in 'debt slavery', saving virtually no money from their work because so much goes back to the moneylender.
● The right to be presumed innocent until proven guilty	● In France the reverse applies. If you are charged with a crime, the responsibility is on you to prove you are innocent. The French claim that their legal system still works, but critics say that it is unfair.
● The right to live in safety and security	● As a result of the ongoing conflict in Israel, Jews and Palestinians live in constant fear of suicide bombings, assassinations, army retaliations, and civil unrest.
● The right to freedom of speech	● People should be able to say what they like. However, in countries such as Peru in South America, right wing militias have terrorised left wing opposition in the past, leading to thousands of people 'disappearing'.
● The right to life	● Although the USA is a signatory to the Universal Declaration of Human Rights, many states in the USA still have the death penalty.

1 **Discuss the statements below. Which do you agree with?**

> "Basic necessities are more important than any other human rights. We should be concentrating on providing food and water where they are needed."
>
> *Zara*

> "All human rights are equally important. What's the use of food and water if you can't live in safety and security?"
>
> *Hamil*

2 **Which human rights do you think are the most important? Why? Give reasons for your views.**

Asylum seekers or economic migrants?

Human rights abuses can force people to leave the country in which they live. A person who has to flee their country is known as a refugee. A refugee may apply for asylum, which is a form of protection that allows the person to stay in another country indefinitely. These people are known as 'asylum seekers'.

In 2002, 84 130 people applied for asylum in the UK. This number had increased by 18% since 2001. Figures have continued to rise in recent years. Asylum seekers are given free accommodation while they make their applications in the UK.

Some asylum seekers enter a country illegally. Most apply for asylum.

However, only 10% of asylum seekers in 2002 were successful. Another 24% were allowed to stay in the UK for a while, and 66% of asylum seekers were refused asylum. Under current rules, they are allowed to appeal against their decision and remain in the UK while doing so.

This has led to concerns that the system of asylum is being exploited by people who simply wish to move to another country in order to improve their standard of living. These people are known as 'economic migrants'. As a result, the government is to review the way the whole asylum system operates.

Human traffic

Economic migration has meant that in the twenty-first century there has been an increase in the crime of human trafficking. Criminal gangs lure people in less developed countries with promises of good jobs and a better life in a more developed country. They then smuggle these people into countries like the UK. Because these people cannot work legally, they are often forced to work for the criminal gangs, i.e. as prostitutes or as slave labour for little or no money.

Which of the statements below do you agree with? Why? Give reasons for your views.

> "If letting in three asylum seekers saves one person from persecution abroad, it's a price worth paying."
>
> *Dominic*

> "People are just coming over here and taking advantage of those of us who were born in the UK."
>
> *Abdul*

> "I'd rather have people here working legitimately than have them being exploited by criminal gangs."
>
> *Lucy*

FOR YOUR FILE

Write a short article on 'economic migration' for an encyclopedia aimed at teenagers. You will need to explain clearly what it is, why it exists, and present some ways you feel it could be controlled.

3 MEDIA MATTERS

Mass media and the news agenda

Aim: To explain how information is conveyed by the mass media, and to explore who controls the news agenda (Citizenship 1g, 2a, 2b, 2c)

The development of the mass media

In the past, the way people received information and news was very different from the way it is received today.

In the nineteenth century, most people received news and information through newspapers or by word of mouth, i.e. people gossiping.

In the twenty-first century, more news is broadcast on TV, radio, the internet and by text message to

Are newspapers old news?

mobile phones than is published in newspapers or spread by gossip. There is also instant access to the news as it happens. Up-to-date news from around the world is available on TV and the internet 24 hours a day. Today's media environment is called the 'mass media'.

Discuss the different ways we receive information and how this has changed over time.

The broadcast media

The broadcast media includes radio and TV. Radio includes national stations that are run by the BBC (British Broadcasting Corporation) and commercial stations that are run privately. In order to broadcast a radio station in the UK, you must have a licence from the government.

TV broadcasting is split into three main sections:

- terrestrial TV
- satellite TV
- digital TV.

Terrestrial TV		Satellite TV	Digital TV
BBC1 and BBC2: The BBC is owned by the UK government but operates independently. This means that whilst the government finances the BBC, it is allowed freedom in what it reports.	ITV, Channel 4 and Channel 5: These commercial stations are privately owned. For example, ITV is made up of a variety of different companies that broadcast to different regions throughout the UK. This allows for regional news coverage and programming. However, two companies – Carlton and Granada – own a number of different TV regions, allowing them greater influence in independent television.	Satellite TV is dominated by Sky, owned by Rupert Murdoch's News International Corporation. This dominant market position, combined with News International's ownership of four newspapers – the *Sun*, *The Times*, *The Sunday Times* and the *News of the World* – means that News International is a key influence when it comes to shaping the UK's news agenda.	This has been a problematic sector, since the collapse of ITV Digital several years ago. The collapse of this pay-tv network had a devastating effect on UK football clubs, which were relying on the success of ITV Digital for revenue. This shows how what goes on in the media industry can have severe effects elsewhere.

Other digital TV channels include ITV2, BBC3 and BBC4. |

What is the cost of greater choice?

Access to some satellite and digital channels comes at a cost. Some stations operate a pay-per-view policy. This means you can pay money to watch a particular football match, much in the same way as you rent a video. Other channels ask you to pay a subscription fee to receive the channel for one year. Supporters of paying for TV argue it extends consumer choice. Critics say that it creates an underclass who cannot afford to watch TV. They argue that this could have an important effect in a democracy. For example, if you have to pay to receive a news TV channel, are people being denied fair access to information?

> "The existence of the BBC is important because it is independent of the government."

> "In a democracy everyone has the right to equal access to news and information so they shouldn't have to pay to receive TV news broadcasts."

> "Multinational corporations, such as News International, should not be allowed to influence the news agenda."

Say why you agree or disagree with the views above.

How powerful is the press?

With the development of the broadcasting media, the importance of the print media has inevitably decreased, yet it still remains powerful in shaping people's opinions. On an average weekday, over half the adult population of the UK read a national daily newspaper. When there is a general election, which political party a newspaper decides to support is therefore very important.

① Do you agree that newspapers shape people's opinions?

② How much influence do you think newspapers have on people's political views – a little or a lot? Say why.

Gatekeepers: people who control the news

There are many news stories that could be included in newspapers, TV, or the radio. A news outlet, such as a newspaper or TV station, has to decide what stories to cover. On a 'fast news day', i.e. a lot of news in 24 hours, it means that there won't be time to cover some stories. On a 'slow news day', stories that are less important are more likely to be published.

A news outlet has to decide how much coverage to give a story. A politician's speech may receive a front page story in one newspaper, only to receive a brief mention inside another newspaper. A news outlet also has to decide what angle or 'spin' to give a story. This can be a positive, negative, supportive, challenging, or critical angle.

These decisions are critical because they influence how people think about a news story. News outlets are deciding what people should know, how important a news story is, and how the story should be interpreted. This is known as acting as a 'gatekeeper'.

The growth in the number of media outlets means that some media power is being diluted. With more text messages and email alerts, other forms of media have to compete for our attention. The more media outlets there are, the less influence an individual outlet has.

However, a growth in the number of media corporations who own large sections of the media, such as Rupert Murdoch's News International, means that together they may be able to influence, or even dictate, the news agenda.

Discuss where you get your news from. Do you have one particular source that you rely on? Do you ever question the accuracy of the news you receive?

FOR YOUR FILE

Choose three front pages from different newspapers for the same day. Compare the news stories they contain. Do they all have the same 'lead' (front page) story? Do they give different amounts of space to the stories? Do they report the stories from the same viewpoint?

Free media

Freedom of speech?

The idea of freedom of speech is key to modern democracy. Article 19 of the Universal Declaration of Human Rights states that: "Everyone has the right to freedom of expression and opinion". In other words, people should be allowed to contribute to a debate – to freely give and receive ideas. This means that the media, where possible, should have as much freedom as is reasonable.

In the USA, there is a completely free media. Anyone can publish or broadcast what they like. For example, if you want to set up a radio station and broadcast your views to the world, there is nothing to stop you from doing so.

In the UK, there are stricter controls. If you want to set up a radio station, you must get a licence from the government. In the USA, you have some radio stations that broadcast extremist views, whilst in the UK a station could be refused a licence if they were suspected of wanting to broadcast racist views.

Controlling the press by limiting information is known as 'censorship'. Some people argue that there ought to be total freedom of the press – people should be able to broadcast, print, read, listen, and watch what they like. Others argue that there should be limits on what the press can do.

Discuss whether you think organisations that promote racist, homophobic or sexist ideas should be allowed to broadcast and publish their views in the UK. Or do you think these organisations should be censored? Give reasons for your views.

Global news networks

In Europe and the USA, a majority of the news comes from a few global news networks. These large news groups include the BBC in the UK, the Associated Press in France, and CNN, ABC and the CBS news networks in the USA.

Critics of these networks claim that because these media groups are based in western, developed countries, they are biased. Thus the global news agenda is slanted towards more developed countries and towards stories and views that are more favourable to the developed world.

However, this has not stopped some groups from getting their message across. During the Second Gulf War (2003–2004), Al Jazeera, an Arabic TV channel based in the Middle East, was used by opponents of western values, such as the terrorist group Al-Qaeda, to get their views across successfully. Western news networks also reported what Al Jazeera had broadcast, and this provided another side to the news and information on the war.

An Al Jazeera broadcast aired during the Second Gulf War

1 Can you think of any examples of bias, where a story has seemed favourable to one particular group or individual? Consider governments, local councils, corporations, pressure groups, and individuals.

2 Is it right that we get most of our news from western news networks?

Spin doctors

Governments, corporations, and pressure groups also employ people to manipulate and influence the media. These people are known as 'spin doctors'. The term comes from America where pitchers try to give a spin to a baseball. The job of a spin doctor is to try to get the media to report a story from a certain angle. Alistair Campbell used to work as a spin doctor for the UK Prime Minister, Tony Blair.

Supporters of spin doctors claim they are necessary to get organisations' messages across, and that they are useful because they provide additional information for a news story. Critics of spin doctors say that they distort stories and lead to a managed news agenda, where it is difficult to see what is really going on.

Spin doctors, like Alistair Campbell, are employed to influence the media

Do you think spin doctors are a good idea? Or do they get in the way of a free media? Give reasons for your views.

Freedom of information

Some countries, such as the USA, have a Freedom of Information Act, which creates a duty for the government to release as much information as possible, whenever possible.

However, this is not the case in the UK, where the government can choose to withhold information. This has a direct effect on the media, which has to search for stories rather than receive some information as a right. This creates an environment that is favourable to the government controlling news agendas.

Should the media ever be controlled?

During the Second World War, the UK government assumed control of the media and decided what stories could or could not be printed. This was done to boost morale in order to help win the war. The government was acting in what is called the 'national interest'. This is the main reason, or excuse, given when a government wants to withhold or release only part of the information that is available to them.

During the Second Gulf War, the UK government was able to influence the news agenda in several different ways. It decided the timing of stories – when to release information, the amount of information it was going to release, and the angle or 'spin' the story was given.

Case study 1

A 15-year-old was recently found guilty of murdering a fellow pupil aged 14. The judge refused to allow the 15-year-old's identity to be released until after the trial because he was a child.

Case study 2

A woman was found guilty of helping her boyfriend who had committed murder. She was convicted of obstructing the course of justice. Because people threatened to kill her, she was given a new identity by the police.

Case study 3

A nuclear accident occurs at a Ministry of Defence site. The government refuses to release full details in order to protect national security.

❶ **Read case study 1. Do you think the judge did the right thing? Why?**

❷ **Read case study 2. Do you think it is right that the press is still not allowed to report her identity? Give reasons for your views.**

❸ **Read case study 3. Do the public have a right to know what is really going on? Why?**

The development of the internet

New technology

Over recent years, developments in technology have affected how people communicate with one another. This new technology includes mobile phones, interactive TV services, digital video recorders, and most importantly, the internet.

The internet in the UK

The internet is a web of global computer connections. It is made up three main parts:

1. Web pages, that provide information for people to read and respond to.
2. Search engines, such as Google, which allow people to find and retrieve information.
3. Email addresses, that provide a point of contact for people to send and receive personal messages.

In the UK, 99% of people use a computer to access the internet, 1% now use mobile phones to get internet access, and 9% use both. This shows the growing importance of mobile phone technology.

Conduct a quick survey in your group to find out:
- Who uses the internet regularly and how do they access it?
- How long do they spend online?
- Which of the four functions (see right) do they use the internet for?
- Compare your results with the rest of the class.

Internet access

In 1998, only 19% of homes in the UK had access to the internet. By 2004, over 50% of UK households had internet access. An increasing number of people – 2.2 million in mid-2003 – now have access to high-speed connections, such as Broadband. This allows a greater number of people to retrieve large documents more quickly.

People in the UK use the internet:
1. for communication, using emails at home, at work, and at school.
2. to access web pages to conduct research and retrieve information.
3. for purchasing goods, services, and for banking – buying 'online'.
4. to surf the web and see what's out there!

The internet: positive or negative?

Supporters of the internet argue that it has transformed the worlds of business, academia, and research. One major advantage of the internet is that it allows access to information quickly and easily. It also allows access to specialist information that may not be readily available elsewhere.

The internet has also broken down the geographical barriers of communication. With email and internet chatrooms, families that have relatives on the other side of the world can now communicate easily. The internet also allows specialist communities to come together with a common interest. There may not be many UFO watchers in Northampton, but across the UK and the world, thousands of UFO watchers can communicate online.

However, the internet has its critics, who believe the spread of information can be dangerous. Author's copyright may be infringed, as people download books, music, and short films without paying. Inappropriate material, such as pornography, may be easily accessible by young children if the proper safeguards aren't in place.

People have also used the internet for illegal purposes. This includes 'hacking' (gaining illegal access to a computer) to get confidential information. Hacking has also been linked to 'cyber-terrorism' – when internet viruses are used to cripple computer networks. Finally, false information can be spread over the internet which can damage companies and people, and create false impressions.

① Use the article to create a list of positive and negative points about the internet.

② Can you think of any other good or bad things about the internet to add to your list? Rank each point in order of importance.

③ Discuss whether you think the internet has had a positive, negative, or neutral impact on society.

The internet in the world: a case of inequality?

In order to gain the positive advantages of the internet, people have to have access to it. One problem is that certain groups of people may have their access limited. In the UK, older people who are less familiar with new technology may have trouble accessing the internet regularly. People who are poor or unemployed often can't afford to use the internet regularly, even though, ironically, many of the best jobs and cheapest deals are advertised on the internet. There is, therefore, a danger that an underclass of people is being created who are unable to access the best information for them.

Looking at the global picture, the problem is even worse. One in two houses might have internet access in the UK, but in some African countries the figure is less than 1 in 1000, and may even be 1 in 10 000. The lack of telephone lines and other ways to access different media means that as technology improves in the developed world, the Third World (or developing world) is being left behind. In addition, 80% of internet sites are written in English. Yet English is only understood by less than 25% of the world's population, creating a language barrier.

1 Discuss what you think life would be like without the internet.

2 How do you think introducing the internet would affect people in a less developed country?

Case study: China

China is a key player in the media industry as the country contains one in four of the world's population. There are 80 million internet users in China, the second largest number per country in the world after the USA. Where people do have internet access, this is tightly controlled by the Chinese government.

The Chinese government censors information in three ways:

In China, access to the internet is tightly controlled by the government

- The publishers of all web pages in China must have a licence from the Chinese government.
- The Chinese government controls the access points where people can access the internet.
- There are strict rules about what political and religious information can be published and accessed in China.

For example, many overseas sites, such as the BBC World Service, cannot be accessed on the internet in China. This is enforced with severe penalties for those who break the rules.

Internet companies which provide web pages in China, such as Yahoo, have been criticised for co-operating with the Chinese government in carrying out this form of censorship because they are providing an internet service that is only available under the Chinese government's conditions. Supporters of the internet in China say that it is better to have some information rather than none at all.

1 Should there be total freedom of speech and access on the internet? Or should there be some form of control?

2 Discuss what sites, if any, you would ban. Give reasons for your views.

4 BUSINESS AND FINANCE

The economy

Aim: To explore how the economy functions, including the role of labour and small businesses (Citizenship 1e, 2a, 2b, 2c)

What is the economy?

The economy of a country is the production and exchange of goods and services, usually for money. The UK economy is made up of all the businesses that operate in the UK. Each of us deals with a variety of different businesses each day. For example, food, paper and pens are all provided by businesses that produce things. Other businesses provide services, such as transport through the use of buses and trains, or financial services that are provided by banks.

In recent years, the number of people working in businesses that make or produce things has declined. By contrast, the number of people working in businesses providing services has increased.

The size of the economy can be measured by adding up the value of all the goods and services produced in a year. This is known as the 'Gross National Product' or GNP of a country. By dividing everything produced in one year, in a country, by the number of people that live there, economists measure a country's wealth. This is known as the average GNP per person in a country.

1 Make a list of all the different goods and services that you have used so far today.

Goods	Services

2 How many goods have you used? How many services? Are you surprised at the length of the list?

The importance of small businesses

Small businesses are particularly important to an economy. Many new ideas, inventions, and services come from small businesses. In the UK, a significant number of jobs are in small businesses that employ 10 people or fewer.

Small businesses are often very dependent on one another. Because of the small amount of goods and services they consume and use, they are vulnerable to fluctuations in the costs of what they use and provide.

Look at the picture of a local high street. Which goods and services do you think are dependent on one another?

Young Enterprise: business in practice

Young Enterprise is a scheme set up by the government to teach students about running a small business. Students set up a company for a term and act as the managers and workers within the company. Ideas have included students printing their own T-shirts, making their own wooden penholders in the CDT department, and providing a car washing service.

Students are encouraged to take on a particular job and thus specialise in one particular area of the company. Each week the company reviews:

- how much money it has spent on producing goods or services
- how much money it has received from selling these goods or services
- how much money the company now has.

The idea is to sell the goods and services for more money than it costs to produce them.

This will lead to the company making a profit (having more money).

In order to make sure the company is a success, students draw up a business plan. This includes:

- who is doing what job
- what costs are likely to be incurred and when
- a marketing plan for promoting the product
- sales targets to be achieved
- how much money will be received and when.

Imagine you are setting up a small business. Would you want to make something or would you prefer to provide a service? Who do you think your main customers would be? Draw up a draft business plan and present it to the rest of the class.

Profit keeps the UK economy healthy

All businesses have to make a profit. By making more money, a firm can reinvest some of the money in their business to make it larger so more goods and services can be produced. This should lead to more profit in the future. This system is known as a 'market economy'.

The economy works because businesses can specialise in one area. For example, a printing company decides to research, write, design, print and distribute a book. However, the company are only really good at printing. It is therefore more efficient to pay an author to research and write the book, use a professional designer to design it, then the company prints it and pays for a distribution company to distribute it. A business can therefore make more money and be more efficient by concentrating on a specific area.

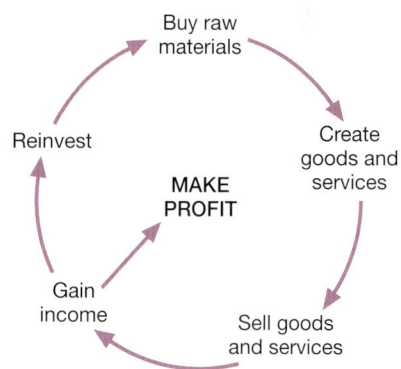

An example of a market economy

Supporters of large businesses say that because they concentrate on one particular area, goods/services can be produced for less money and therefore they can be sold more cheaply, which is good for the consumer/user – you!

However, critics of large businesses say that sometimes they can become too powerful. This is because they can purchase their raw materials more cheaply in bulk. Smaller businesses suffer because they cannot do this. For example, a corner shop cannot afford to price its goods as cheaply as a large supermarket. A large factory can produce goods more cheaply than a small manufacturing firm.

Larger businesses may also have different goals to the economy of a local area. For example, to save money, a company may close down a factory in one area, and expand a factory in another. This means that one of the two areas loses out and jobs are lost.

1 **Discuss how the market economy works. If a business concentrates on one area, how does this lead to the growth of larger businesses?**

2 **What effect does the growth of large businesses have on smaller businesses?**

3 **How can the decisions made by larger businesses affect the local economy of an area?**

How the UK economy works

Aim: To discuss how the economy is managed by the government, including fighting inflation and unemployment (Citizenship 1e, 2a, 2b, 2c)

The public and private sector

The UK economy can be divided into two parts:

1. The private sector, which includes privately owned companies which are trying to make a profit, such as British Gas, Lloyds TSB Bank, or Virgin Trains.

2. The public sector, which contains everything that is owned by the government on behalf of the public. This includes the Armed Forces, and the majority of schools and hospitals. About 40% of the economy is in the public sector.

Economic growth, inflation and unemployment

The government's main aim is to control the amount the economy grows. In achieving economic growth, the government has to balance two factors:

- inflation
- unemployment.

Discuss what is meant by inflation and unemployment. Which do you think is more important – fighting inflation or fighting unemployment? Give reasons for your views.

Inflation is the amount prices rise each year. Fighting inflation is important because many people have fixed incomes. As prices rise, the amount they earn stays fixed. This means during times when prices rise rapidly, these people lose out.

Unemployment is the number of people of working age who do not have a job. There is a natural amount of unemployment in any economy – usually about 5% of the workforce – as people move between jobs. Fighting unemployment reduces poverty and crime, and reduces the amount of money the government has to pay to people who are out of work.

The role of the banking sector

The role of the banking sector plays an important part in managing the UK economy. Banks have several functions. They either lend money or let people save money with them. In each case, banks charge interest on the amount borrowed, or add interest to the amount saved. This means the amount borrowed or saved grows.

However, lending lots of money can cause problems. People may not be able to pay back the interest. This means a person or a company can run out of money if they are unable to afford the payments.

The Bank of England influences the economy by setting 'interest rates' which are the cost of borrowing money. By raising interest rates, the cost of borrowing goes up. This encourages people to borrow less money and spend less, which slows down growth in the economy. Lower interest rates encourages spending and speeds the economy up.

However, a higher interest rate may mean that more small businesses cannot afford to borrow money. This means that they can no longer employ people, which causes unemployment.

Imagine you are company directors who have borrowed £100 000 to set up a business. How much money will you have to pay back if the interest rate is 5%? Or 10%? Discuss what effect raising interest rates has on the cost of borrowing.

Government taxation

The government also uses how it collects and spends money to control the economy. The way the government collects money is known as taxation.

1. Direct taxation Income tax is a form of direct taxation. This is when the government takes money directly from people's wages. The amount of income tax paid depends on the amount of money earned. Everyone in the UK is allowed to earn £4800 before they are taxed. Most people pay an income tax of around 20% of what they earn. However, if you earn more than £36 000, you pay an income tax of 40%. Businesses also pay tax on the profits they make.

People also pay direct taxation in the form of National Insurance, or NI, which represents around 9% of an income. This tax provides people with insurance, for instance if you are injured at work.

2. Indirect taxation Indirect taxation is money paid to the government indirectly, i.e. from a tax on goods or services. The main form of indirect taxation is Value Added Tax or VAT. On most goods and services in the UK we pay an extra 17.5% in VAT. Some goods, such as books, food, and children's clothes, are not taxable.

Other forms of indirect taxation include council tax, which each household in the UK pays depending on how much their house or flat is worth. This money is used to help finance local government.

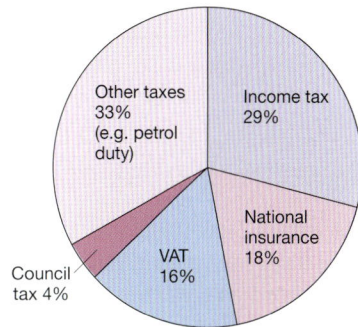

This pie chart shows the amount of money the government raises in direct and indirect taxation

UK GOVERNMENT REVENUE, 2003–4

Supporters think that direct taxation is fairer because people pay roughly according to how much they can afford to pay. This usually helps people on smaller incomes. Critics think that indirect taxation is fairer and that people should pay according to how much they consume. This usually helps people who consume less or who are on larger incomes.

❶ **Imagine you are the government. Create a pie chart reflecting how you would raise your revenue. How much will you raise from different types of taxation?**

❷ **Compare your pie chart with the pie chart above. Where are they similar/different?**

Government expenditure

Government expenditure can boost different parts of the UK economy. For instance, during the Second Iraq War (2003–2004), the government temporarily increased the amount it spent on military equipment.

There are many different areas on which the government spends money. The biggest area is Social Security, i.e. providing benefits to people who are ill, sick, or out of work. In 2003–2004, this was 29% of government expenditure.

The person in control of government expenditure and taxation is the Chancellor of the Exchequer. Once a year, the Chancellor will set out taxation and spending plans for the following year. This is known as the budget and it happens every March.

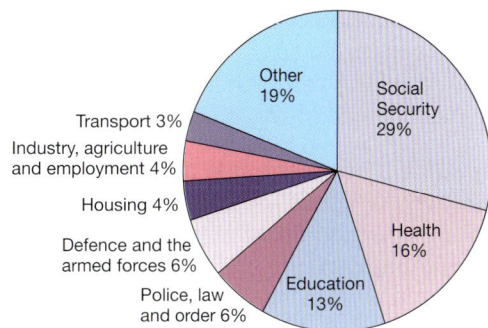

The amount of government expenditure in 2003–2004 in different areas

UK GOVERNMENT EXPENDITURE, 2003–4

Imagine you are the government. Draw a pie chart reflecting how you would spend money to boost different parts of the economy. Compare your pie chart with the pie chart above. Where are they similar? Where are they different?

5 THE GLOBAL ECONOMY

Globalisation and trade

Aim: To examine what globalisation means, and how businesses and countries trade with one another (Citizenship 1e, 2a, 2b, 2c)

How the global economy works

The global economy works like the UK national economy, but on a much larger scale. In the same way that different firms specialise in certain goods and services, so different countries have particular strengths in different industries. For example, Switzerland is famous for its financial services, the UK is a world leader in biotechnology, and much of the world's coffee comes from South America.

Can you think of any other examples of countries that specialise in certain goods and services? What is Japan famous for? How about China or India?

Globalisation

Globalisation is the rise in interdependence between countries and companies. This means that both become more dependent or reliant on one another. As companies and countries specialise in different goods and services, they achieve larger economies of scale. This means, that on a global scale, companies and countries can save millions of pounds by specialising in certain areas. This has been the main driving force of economic growth around the world since the Second World War.

However, at the same time companies and countries also lose the ability to produce other goods and services. This means that a problem in one company or country can have wide far-reaching effects. For example, Saudi Arabia produces a lot of oil. However, if there is terrorist activity in Saudi Arabia, the price of oil will rise. This will affect all those countries that use oil, such as the UK and USA, i.e. for petrol. This makes it more expensive to transport goods in the UK and USA, and as a result the price of goods manufactured in these countries will also rise.

Imagine a hurricane hits a coffee-producing country. Which other countries, as well as that country, would be affected by this? What would happen?

This Caribbean island was hit by a hurricane and the tourist industry was wiped out

Economic development

Specialisation works because of a system of free trade. This free movement of goods and services allows companies to achieve a profit without restriction. This system encourages economic growth, with profit as the driving force behind it.

However, because of the size of the global economy, different areas benefit or lose out. Richer countries that have developed their economies are growing richer. These are known as More Economically Developed Countries (MEDCs) and include the UK, USA, nearly all of the EU, and Japan.

LEDCs are Less Economically Developed Countries. These include countries such as the Sudan in Africa, and Afghanistan in Asia. These countries are becoming relatively poorer as the more developed countries continue to grow.

However, there are some countries that do not fall into either category. One example is China. China now has a massively growing economy, with a booming manufacturing sector. This is because China is in the middle of an industrial and telecommunications revolution, which is changing the economy rapidly.

Look at a map of the world. Which countries would you say are MEDCs? Which countries are LEDCs? Are there any countries like China that are difficult to classify? Compare your ideas with other pairs.

Free trade versus fair trade

One of the causes of the difference in wealth between more and less economically developed countries is the way that profit is distributed when goods and services are manufactured and sold.

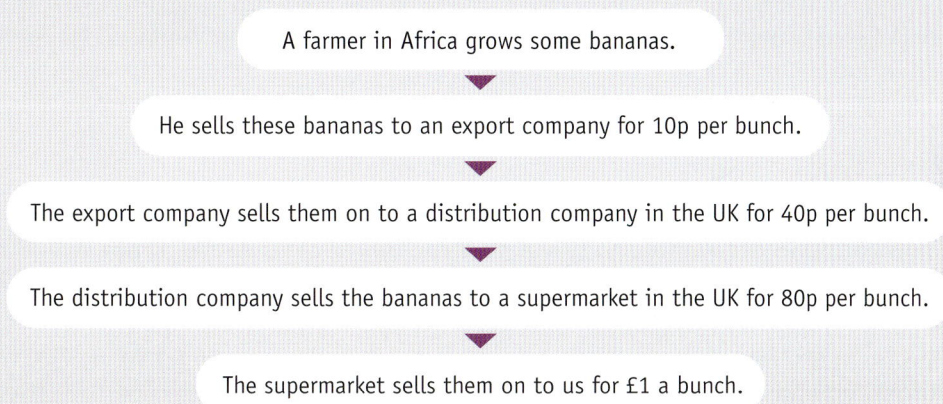

A farmer in Africa grows some bananas.

▼

He sells these bananas to an export company for 10p per bunch.

▼

The export company sells them on to a distribution company in the UK for 40p per bunch.

▼

The distribution company sells the bananas to a supermarket in the UK for 80p per bunch.

▼

The supermarket sells them on to us for £1 a bunch.

Flowchart showing the way profit is distributed when goods are manufactured and sold

In the example above, the farmer receives 10% of the revenue, the export company receives 30%, the distribution company gets 40%, and the supermarket company gets 20%.

The export company, distribution company, and supermarkets are able to do this because of their strong market positions. But because the export companies all charge the same amount of money, the farmer has no choice but to accept their prices.

Fair trade

Fair trade is about increasing the power of ordinary workers in less developed countries. This works by forming workers into co-operatives. Thus, all the banana farmers in an area will group together. They can then demand a higher price for their bananas from the export company, or even contact the distribution company directly. As a result they may be able to achieve 40p per bunch of bananas they sell, as opposed to 10p per bunch previously, thus greatly increasing their income.

Fair trade can also be used to encourage environmental protection, e.g. only accepting banana farmers into the co-operative who do not use chemicals when growing their crops.

Discuss the advantages and disadvantages of fair trade and free trade. Draw a table summarising this.

Labour exploitation: economic slavery

Sometimes a worker producing goods receives virtually no money. An example is workers in South-East Asia that stitch footballs. They worked for long hours for only a few pence, while the footballs were sold for several pounds in more developed countries, making large profits for the companies involved.

Third World debt

What is Third World debt?

The term 'First World' refers to more developed countries such as the USA, the UK, and Japan. The 'Second World' is used to refer to the former USSR and other Communist countries before the collapse of Communism. The 'Third World' includes the less developed countries of the world, particularly in Africa and Asia. 'Third World debt' refers to large amounts of money borrowed by less developed countries.

Debt is the amount of money you owe someone. For example, you may borrow £100 from your bank to buy a new bicycle. In a year's time, because the interest rate is 5%, you pay the bank back £105. The cost of borrowing the money is thus £5.

However, if interest rates are higher, the cost of borrowing goes up. If interest rates were 10%, you would have to pay back £110 to buy your bicycle. The cost of borrowing would therefore have doubled to £10.

On a global scale, this can have enormous consequences. Third World countries have borrowed billions of pounds, when interest rates were low. But because interest rates can rise, the cost of borrowing money can go up significantly.

1 Imagine your parents wanted to buy a new car, which costs £5000. What would the cost of borrowing be over one year if interest rates were: (a) 5%, (b) 10%, and (c) 20%?

2 Now imagine they had to pay the interest each year. What would the cost of borrowing be at 5% interest over (a) three years, (b) five years, and (c) 10 years? (Don't forget, you have to add the interest on each year.)

How was Third World debt created?

In the early 1970s, the world enjoyed a long period of economic growth. More developed countries had lots of excess money. Their banks lent money to less developed countries in the Third World. The idea was to fund economic growth in less developed countries.

However, there were a lot of problems in less developed countries. Sometimes this was due to natural disasters, like widespread flooding in Bangladesh, which destroyed crops and therefore much of the country's economy. In other cases, like Mozambique, a long civil war drained the country of its resources, with money being spent on defence and arms rather than economic growth. In other countries, like Niger, fluctuations in world trade meant that the cost of the raw materials it produced, like uranium, were worth less on the world market. Finally, countries like Iraq had a lack of democracy that meant the government borrowed the money and then simply spent it on what it liked, such as weapons research or lavish palaces for its dictators, rather than on economic development.

In Iraq the government borrowed money to fund economic growth and misspent it

All of these factors meant that these countries were short of money and are now in debt. When interest rates rose at the end of the 1970s, they found their debt repayments rising. However, these countries were unable to afford these payments. As they were countries, not companies, it was impossible to become bankrupt.

These countries thus borrowed more money, simply to meet their interest repayments. These of course then rose further. However, the economic growth in the Third World has not kept up with the growth in interest payments and debt. Thus, much of the Third World has rising debts with no real way of escaping the problem.

Draw a flowchart to show how Third World debt occurs, including examples where possible.

What sorts of problems does Third World debt cause?

Third World debt is damaging because it causes the governments of less developed countries to search for alternative ways of paying off their debts. This can be very damaging to the environment, as countries exploit their rich natural resources such as their trees, minerals or oil. Because they are only interested in profit, these governments cannot afford to think about the long-term environmental damage they are doing to their own countries.

In countries such as Afghanistan in Asia today, and Colombia in South America in the past, the government has illegally supported the drugs trade to help generate money in its economy. Whilst this helps reduce debt repayment, it creates an economic dependency on the drugs industry, ruining public health, and reducing democracy as the drug barons corrupt the countries politicians.

Sometimes, banks and governments in more developed countries can make the problem worse. They may reduce the debt, but insist on harsh economic reforms in return. For example, this often means less developed countries save money by reducing government spending on education and healthcare in areas of the world that most need it.

Discuss the problems that Third World debt causes. Which do you think is the worst problem caused by Third World debt? Give reasons for your views.

Drop the debt

Jubilee 2000 is an example of an international pressure group (see page 40). Its main aim is to cancel much of the debt of the world's 50 poorest countries. It contains over 90 different organisations from around the world, including various religious groups, and local and national pressure groups, such as Oxfam and the TUC.

International pressure group Jubilee 2000 works to help reduce Third World debt

Jubilee 2000 has had amazing success in recent years, with countries such as the USA, UK, and Canada all agreeing to reduce significantly the amount of debt that Third World countries owe them. However, in many cases, they have imposed terms and conditions on these countries. Also, the more developed countries may choose to reduce or write off certain debts – such as those that support their arms industry (see page 32), encouraging the Third World country to buy more arms in the future.

Imagine the UK was in debt and you have to cut government spending. What would you do to save money? Would you reduce spending on the education system, the NHS or recycling schemes? What else would you do?

6 GLOBAL CHALLENGES

Wars, weapons and terrorism

Aim: To understand the arms trade, what weapons of mass destruction are and how they affect the world (Citizenship 1j, 2a, 2b, 2c)

What is the arms trade?

The arms trade is the production and sale of all weapons and military equipment that are used by armies around the world. Almost £1000 billion a year is spent on arms, which represents around 3% of the world's production of all goods.

Critics argue that the arms trade is damaging for three reasons.

1. It causes human misery through all the lives that are lost, people who are injured and the destruction that results from the use of weapons in wars.
2. It means that countries are more tempted to resolve situations by violence, rather than co-operating with one another.
3. It prevents money from being spent on other areas, such as education and health.

Arms are bought and sold through trade fairs

The arms race

In less developed countries, over £140 billion is spent on arms each year. This is usually a result of an 'arms race'. This is when a group of countries each tries to build up the largest army and greatest amount of weapons.

For instance, one country starts to buy military equipment and increases the size of its armed forces. Neighbouring countries get worried, so they increase the size of their armed forces. As the problem spreads, countries spend more and more trying to outdo one another.

This has occurred in many regions of the world, particularly in parts of Africa. Arms races have also taken place between the USA and the USSR from 1960–80, and between India and Pakistan in 2000.

❶ **Discuss what is meant by the term 'arms race'.**

❷ **Imagine you were the government of a small, less developed country in Africa and your neighbours started increasing the size of their army. Would you increase the size of your defence forces, even if it meant cutting money from health or education? Or would you rely on the protection of larger, more developed countries like the USA? Give reasons for your views.**

The arms trade in the UK

The UK is the second largest exporter of arms after the USA. Each year millions of pounds worth of military equipment is exported from the UK. The government supports the arms industry in several ways:

- By giving grants to help build arms factories in areas of high unemployment.
- By holding trade fairs for less developed countries to encourage them to buy arms.
- By helping UK arms firms market their products with government support.
- By providing loans for less developed countries that cannot afford to buy arms immediately.
- By providing debt relief, which reduces Third World debt (see page 31) so that there is more money to be spent on UK arms exports.

A free market for the arms trade

A major problem facing the UK is that there is a free market in the arms trade, i.e. any country can produce and sell weapons and military equipment. Supporters of the arms trade argue that if the UK does not sell arms to a country, another producer of arms will. This means that the UK will lose out if it refuses to manufacture and sell arms to other countries.

Certain groups, like CAAT (Campaign Against the Arms Trade), argue that what is needed is an ethical foreign policy from a number of governments. This would mean that governments in more developed countries with arms industries would refuse to sell arms to dictators and to countries where arms may be used aggressively, rather than as a means of defence. Groups like CAAT argue that if more developed countries acted together, they could significantly reduce the arms trade around the world.

1 **Discuss the statements below, saying why you agree or disagree with them.**

"The UK should only manufacture arms for use by British forces or our allies."

"Until other countries agree to stop manufacturing and selling arms, we should go on doing so."

"The arms trade is immoral. We shouldn't sell arms to countries that are engaged in conflicts or where there are dictators in power."

2 **On what ideas should an ethical foreign policy be based? Give reasons for your views.**

Weapons of mass destruction

Weapons of mass destruction are weapons that can kill people in very large numbers. These weapons were invented or developed for widespread use in the 20th century. They are outlawed because of the extremely large number of people that they can kill indiscriminately. Here are some examples:

Biological weapons

These were the first type of weapon of mass destruction to be developed easily since they occur naturally. Biological weapons rely on infecting people with deadly germs to kill them. Modern potential biological weapons include anthrax, botulism, and the ebola virus.

Chemical weapons

Chemical weapons involve the use of toxic chemicals to kill or disable. They were first widely used in the First World War when chemicals like chlorine were added to mustard gas. As a result of the horrific injuries suffered by people during the First World War, the Geneva Convention of 1925 banned all chemical weapons. However, the Iraqi dictator Saddam Hussein used chemical weapons on his own people in the late 1980s in order to crush opposition to his rule.

Nuclear weapons

These weapons were developed during the Second World War. In 1945 the USA dropped two nuclear bombs on the Japanese cities of Hiroshima and Nagasaki, in order to force the Japanese to surrender. A nuclear explosion causes a huge fireball that kills everyone nearby and makes an area uninhabitable for many years to come. This is due to radioactive contamination.

New weapons of mass destruction

Following the events of September 11 2001 in the USA (see page 35), terrorists proved that there were now new weapons of mass destruction. By using passenger aircraft as missiles, the terrorists were able to kill thousands of people as the chemical fuel in the planes exploded on impact with densely populated buildings.

Which do you think poses the greatest threat to humanity – biological, chemical or nuclear weapons? Give reasons for your views.

FOR YOUR FILE

Write a letter to a newspaper expressing your views on the dangers of weapons of mass destruction.

Terrorism

Aim: To discuss what terrorism is, what causes and maintains it, and how terrorism can be fought (Citizenship 1j, 2a, 2b, 2c)

What is terrorism and how is it caused?

Terrorists are people who want some sort of change. What makes them different from politicians and pressure groups is that they use violence to achieve their goals. This violence then causes extreme fear or terror, hence the term 'terrorist'.

The use of terrorism has existed for hundreds of years. However, because it is now so easy to travel between countries, terrorists can now operate across the world.

Terrorists are extreme people driven to extreme actions. People choose to become terrorists when they feel that there is no alternative to get their message across, or nothing will happen if they don't commit acts of violence. They believe that the end justifies the means.

Terrorism is also more likely to occur when people feel their lives have no value. In some extreme cases, people are willing to sacrifice their own lives for their cause.

Terrorists holding people hostage during the war in Iraq 2003–4

What keeps terrorism going and how to stop it

Below are some reasons why terrorism continues and suggestions for ways to stop it.

1. The cycle of violence

One group decides to use violence to achieve its ends and innocent people are killed or injured. Then the other side starts using violence and the situation spirals. One way to stop the cycle of violence is the intervention of a third party to achieve conflict resolution. Sometimes, a 'ceasefire' (when two sides stop fighting) is called. This has been tried many times during the war between Israel and Palestine (1967–present day), but terrorist attacks keep restarting.

2. Stereotyping

Stereotyping is when people are only identified as being part of a certain group and that all people in that group behave in a certain way. An example of stereotyping is saying that in Northern Ireland all Protestants treat Catholics unfairly or all Catholics support the IRA. Stereotyping can be fought when people are treated as individuals and it is recognised that people behave in different ways.

3. Injustice

If one group can get away with crimes, its opposition will have no respect for the law. For example, if the government in Pakistan uses violence to stop its opponents from speaking out, it only helps the terrorists to justify their actions. A solution would be to create a rule of law that everyone is treated fairly.

4. Weapons

If people have weapons, they are more likely to commit violence. Disarmament is a key way to reduce terrorism and violence.

5. Economic conditions

People fight when they feel desperate. If there is economic growth and stability, people will have less reason to fight. There are fewer terrorist organisations in more economically developed countries that have a fair distribution of wealth.

Using the points above, discuss what you think is the main reason for terrorism continuing today. What is the best way to stop terrorism? Give reasons for your views.

What do terrorists fight for?

Terrorists fight for some sort of aim, known as a 'cause'. This usually involves wanting a political change. Some terrorist groups are fighting to try to establish their own countries and governments. For instance, the Kurdish Liberation Front (KLF) is fighting for the establishment of a country called Kurdistan (see right). This is to unite the Kurdish people who live in southeast Turkey and northwest Iraq as a result of a dispute over the borders that were drawn up between these countries after the Second World War.

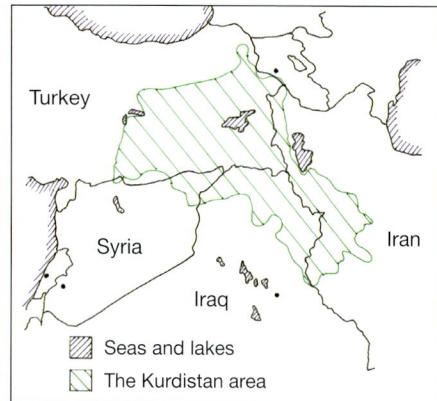

Turkey

Syria

Iran

Iraq

▨ Seas and lakes
◳ The Kurdistan area

Other terrorist groups are fighting to change the balance of power in the world. Groups such as Al-Qaeda have claimed a holy war against the USA, with the aim of creating chaos in the Middle East in order to reduce America's power and influence in the region.

During the Second World War some groups undertook terrorist activity in order to fight Nazi atrocities. Do you think there is ever a case where terrorist activity can be justified?

Case study: 11 September 2001

On 11 September 2001, the terrorist group Al-Qaeda managed to hijack several planes inside the USA. Two of them were crashed in New York, destroying the World Trade Centre. In total, thousands of people died in the attacks.

In response, the US President George W Bush declared 'a war on terror'. The UK government, led by Tony Blair, supported this. The US and UK governments authorised the invasion of Afghanistan where the Al-Qaeda leader, Osama Bin Laden, was hiding. The Afghanistan Government was overthrown, but Bin Laden escaped.

In 2003, the USA linked the leader of Iraq, Saddam Hussein, to Al-Qaeda. It was also claimed that Iraq was hiding weapons of mass destruction (see page 33). Iraq was invaded by a group of countries led by the USA and the UK. However, the weapons of mass destruction have never been found and the links between Saddam Hussein and Al-Qaeda were proved to be minimal.

Supporters of this military action say that the terrorists need to be taught a lesson. Also they claim that terrorists no longer have the support of the governments of Afghanistan or Iraq.

Critics of war say that all the USA and UK have done is create a stronger breeding ground for terrorism. This is because the presence of foreign troops in countries like Iraq is offensive to many Muslims.

❶ Were the USA and the UK right to respond to the events of 11 September by taking military action?

❷ Say why you agree or disagree with each of the statements below.

> "We were right to hunt down the terrorists. We were not right to start a war in Iraq. That has only encouraged more terrorists around the world."

> "I wish we spent as much money on solving conflict and promoting peace as we did on the wars in Iraq and Afghanistan. Then, perhaps, there would be fewer terrorists in the first place."

7 ENVIRONMENTAL ISSUES

Environmental issues

Aim: To explore sustainable development and the main ways it could be applied around the world (Citizenship 1j, 2a, 2b, 2c)

The economy and the environment

Since the industrial revolution started in the UK in the 1700s, economic development around the world has accelerated. As a result, this has often meant that the environment has not been protected when developments have occurred. This means there are now several human-made threats to our environment that are occurring across the world. These include:

- **Global warming:** Gases released by industries and vehicles using natural resources mean that more carbon dioxide gas (CO_2) is now present in the Earth's atmosphere. This traps more of the sun's energy, causing the planet to heat up. This leads to a rise in sea levels, extensive flooding, and extreme weather conditions.

- **Pollution:** More of our natural environment is becoming polluted with chemicals from human activities, such as industry. Air pollution from traffic is one of the main causes of asthma in the UK today. Meanwhile, chemicals entering our water cause acid rain that is damaging trees and forests, and contributes to species extinction.

- **Species extinction:** More of the natural environment is destroyed when forests are cut down, roads are created, and more houses are built. This leaves less natural land for other living creatures, leading to a loss of biodiversity (the number of different living species in an area). In some cases, plants and animals die out. This is known as species extinction.

The giant panda faces extinction as more of its natural environment is destroyed

Which of these human-made problems poses the most threat to the environment in the UK? What do you think we can do to help the situation? Give reasons for your views.

Sustainable development

Sustainable development is different from economic development. This is because development still occurs, but only when it does not damage the environment. Sustainable development requires three main factors to be considered:

1. That scarce natural resources are not wasted and natural alternatives are used where possible.

2. That the environment is not damaged, now or in the future.

3. That it is actually achievable in the long term. For example, whilst we could all stop driving cars overnight, we would need an alternative form of transport.

Sustainable solutions around the world

Sustainable development needs to take place on a global scale in order to make a real difference. There are three main areas where this is needed:

1. Energy consumption

Much of our energy consumption comes from burning scarce natural resources, such as wood in less developed countries, and oil, coal and gas in more developed countries.

One solution in more developed countries has been to use nuclear energy. This is cheap and does not produce any gases that contribute to global warming. However, nuclear energy produces waste material that remains dangerous because it is radioactive for hundreds of years.

Two other alternatives are wind and wave power. Turbines are used to harvest natural energy from the wind and from the waves in the sea. Denmark now produces over 50% of its electricity in this way. However, this often means building large wind turbines in areas of natural beauty (see right).

2. Food consumption

Vast amounts of food are consumed across the world. Yet the intensive growing of crops to meet this demand often damages the soil. The use of pesticides to increase the amount of food grown can increase chemical pollution.

One solution has been to develop genetically modified (GM) crops that use less pesticides. Supporters of GM crops say they are environmentally friendly. However, critics argue that the long-term effects of GM crops are not known.

3. Protecting natural resources

Wood is a scare natural resource that is being used up rapidly around the planet. Cutting down trees for wood leads to deforestation, particularly in places like South America. This leads to a loss of biodiversity, and increases species extinction and global warming.

One solution is sustainable forestry – replanting trees to replace those that are cut down. However, new trees can take years to grow.

Decide on four reasons why you support or oppose (a) the development of a wind farm on a hillside near your home; and (b) a farmer growing GM crops in fields near where you live.

Sustainable development in less developed countries

By economically developing to fight poverty, less developed countries exploit their natural resources which increases pollution (see page 31). More developed countries, like the USA and UK, want this development to be sustainable.

However, critics say that more developed countries should first clean up their own act. For example, the USA uses 40% of the world's energy resources. The biggest change that could be made to the environment would be the USA reducing its energy consumption.

"It is hypocritical of us to tell less developed countries that they have to stick to sustainable development, when more developed countries don't clean up their own act."

"We should be doing more to help less developed countries undertake sustainable development. After all, it's in our interests, as well as theirs."

FOR YOUR FILE

Copy these two statements and say whether you agree or disagree with each of them in at least two sentences.

Local environmental issues

Think globally, act locally

In the 21st century, there are a large number of different environmental problems to sort out. This requires co-operation at all levels – locally, nationally, and internationally. The UK government is encouraging local councils to have local initiatives to help sort out particular environmental problems in their area.

A key part of this is Agenda 21. This is a global plan to protect and improve the earth's environment for the 21st century. Agenda 21 was agreed at a United Nations summit on the Environment, held in Rio De Janeiro in 1992.

The central idea is to encourage people locally to take action. This means that community-based projects will be created that are led by people in their local community.

Different issues that could be tackled under Agenda 21

These include:

- traffic congestion
- graffiti
- recycling
- getting rid of abandoned cars
- sorting out parking problems
- reducing energy consumption from local houses and businesses.

1 **Which of the above issues are problems in your local area?**

2 **How do you think each of these things could be sorted out using local solutions?**

3 **Draw up ideas to add into the Agenda 21 action plan for your area. Then share your ideas in a class discussion.**

FOR YOUR FILE

Research and write a short report about what your local council is doing to solve the environmental problems in your area.

Focus on: dealing with the rubbish

In the UK, large amounts of rubbish are buried in the ground, or burnt which causes air pollution. A key issue is, therefore, how much waste we need to recycle. Different cities around the world have come up with different solutions:

- In Bournemouth, there is a blue bag scheme for recycling. People can put paper, bottles and plastics into the blue bag, which is then collected with the ordinary rubbish. The material from the blue bag is recycled and materials reused. The blue bag scheme is run in partnership with Oxfam, who then use the money from selling the recycled materials to help people in less developed countries.

- In Oxford, there are separate street bins for three types of rubbish in the city centre. You have to put glass and cans in one bin, paper in another, and the remaining rubbish in the third. This makes it easier for the council to recycle the rubbish.

- In Toronto, Canada, it is illegal to throw away glass bottles that could be recycled. This encourages people to take their bottles to a bottle bank, where they can be recycled.

Recycling by a local council

What sort of recycling facilities exist in your local area? Do you think it should be illegal not to recycle your rubbish? Give reasons for your views.

Focus on: reducing energy consumption

Reducing the amount of energy we use means that we reduce pollution caused by generating energy. These are some of the methods that have been used internationally to reduce the amount of energy used:

- In Australia, new apartment blocks have solar power to provide them with hot water. This means that electricity and gas bills are reduced, as solar power is a form of sustainable energy.
- In Chicago, buildings have rooftop gardens. These keep the heat off the building, thus reducing electricity required for air conditioning. The plants in these gardens also reduce CO_2 gases.
- In London, using battery-powered vehicles is encouraged. These create no noise and no air pollution. The battery-powered vehicles can only travel up to 40mph, which is faster than most London traffic!

Battery-powered vehicles in London

Imagine you had to design a building in your local area. List the features that you would include to make it environmentally friendly.

Focus on: cleaning up the local area

Improving the environment also means keeping an area neat and tidy. Some ways to encourage this include:

- clearing up abandoned vehicles. In Kingston, South London, the local council has formed a partnership with the local police. Any abandoned vehicles are quickly removed and scrapped, and as much material is recycled as possible.
- zero tolerance. In the US in the late 1990s, the Mayor of New York introduced a zero tolerance policy where the police would arrest and prosecute people for the most minor crime, including dropping litter and drinking in public areas where drinking was forbidden. This saw a decrease in crime across the city and a 'clean up' of the area.

Discuss whether you think zero tolerance should be introduced in your local area. Do you think it is right that the police should arrest people for dropping litter if it helps clean up the environment?

Do we need stronger rules to protect our environment?

After the 1992 United Nations summit in Rio de Janeiro, it became apparent that not enough progress was being made to protect the environment. As a result, five years later the Kyoto Summit was held in Japan to follow up on the work of the Rio Summit. However, in 1999 the new US president, George W Bush, decided the USA did not agree with the Kyoto Summit's recommendations, despite the fact that the USA consumes a large proportion of the world's energy and so causes much of the world's pollution.

Environmentalists argue that stronger action is needed to protect the world's environment. At an international level, this means forcing the USA to face up to its responsibilities. At a local level, this means we take responsibility for our own actions. The key idea is that 'the polluter' pays. This would mean that the USA pays for the CO_2 pollution that it creates, and local people pay for the amount of rubbish each household produces.

Do you think that households should pay for each tonne of rubbish that they produce? Or do you think each individual should pay a certain amount for the rubbish they throw away? Give reasons for your views.

8 WORKING FOR CHANGE

International pressure groups

Aim: To understand what international pressure groups are, what issues they campaign on, and what campaign methods they use (Citzenship 1f, 2a, 2b, 2c, 3b, 3c)

What are international pressure groups?

International pressure groups are similar to local or national pressure groups, except that they operate on a much larger scale.

They can be sectional – representing the wide interests of a particular section of society. For example, the International Trade Union Movement campaigns to advance the interests of all of its members worldwide.

Local and national pressure groups concentrate on specific areas of policy. However, international pressure groups may campaign on a range of different but connected issues. For example, the international pressure group Greenpeace looks at everything that affects the environment on a global scale.

The issues that international pressure groups campaign on tend to be more complicated, such as world peace, tackling world poverty, or fighting the spread of AIDS. As a result they often have large memberships that span many countries. International pressure groups will also run bigger, high profile, and longer campaigns.

In addition to targeting national governments to try to influence their policies, international pressure groups target international institutions. These can be groups of countries, for instance the European Union (EU) or the Organisation of Petroleum Exporting

International pressure group Greenpeace campaigns on a global scale

Countries (OPEC) which produce most of the world's oil.

Other international institutions targeted are organisations such as the World Bank or the International Monetary Fund (IMF), which make decisions that affect the world's economy, or the North Atlantic Treaty Organisation (NATO), which works to maintain world peace.

International pressure groups also target big businesses, in particular multinational corporations, such as Nike, McDonald's and BP. These companies are spread over many countries and wield enormous economic power.

① **Discuss what you have learned about international pressure groups.**

② **List the differences between local pressure groups and international pressure groups. What are the similarities between the two groups?**

The antiglobalisation movement

International pressure groups may come together to form a 'coalition' – working together to try to achieve a common aim. This has been made much easier by the growth of the internet, which allows groups in different countries to contact each other, regardless of international boundaries.

An example of a coalition is the antiglobalisation movement, which protests against the economic, social and environmental damage that world economic growth causes around the world today. The coalition includes environmental pressure groups, some Trade Unions, left-wing pressure groups and anarchists (people who are opposed to authority, such as governments).

The antiglobalisation movement's most successful tactic has been to organise mass protests wherever governments from more developed countries, and financial institutions, such as the World Trade Organisation, have met. As a result, such meetings are now being held in remote areas.

Design a poster to be used by an international pressure group. What slogan will you use? What image will you use?

International pressure group issues

Below are the four main groups of issues on which international pressure groups are campaigning today, along with an example of each group.

Economic issues

These include:

1. **Reducing world poverty.** In particular, reducing the poverty of some less developed countries where people live on less than 60p a day. **International pressure group:** War on Want

2. **Eliminating Third World debt** (see page 30), so that Third World countries are not continually paying back interest on outstanding money they have borrowed. **International pressure group:** Jubilee 2000

3. **Fair trade instead of free trade.** This is where goods are produced without workers being exploited. **International pressure group:** The Fairtrade Foundation

Conflict issues

Conflict issues arise out of wars and conflicts around the world today. Issues campaigned on include:

7. **The arms trade.** Many international pressure groups argue that governments should spend less on arms and more on other areas. **International pressure group:** Campaign Against the Arms Trade (CAAT)

8. **Nuclear weapons.** A variety of international pressure groups exist that believe nuclear weapons are dangerous and should be banned and destroyed. **International pressure group:** Campaign for Nuclear Disarmament (CND)

9. **Landmines.** When a war is over, landmines are often left which cause death and serious injury for many years afterwards. **International pressure group:** Oxfam

Environmental issues

These are all interlinked, as one environmental issue often connects to another.

4. **Access to clean water.** Millions of people currently live without access to a clean water supply. **International pressure group:** Water Aid

5. **Global warming.** The threat of global warming can lead to loss of land, changing weather patterns, and displacement of people. **International pressure group:** Friends of the Earth

6. **Species extinction.** This is when a particular animal dies out and becomes extinct. On a large scale, extinction has serious consequences. For example, if many species of fish become extinct, an important food supply is lost. **International pressure group:** World Wildlife Fund (WWF)

Social issues

Social issues affect the way that we choose to live. Examples of important social issues include:

10. **Discrimination.** Many international human rights pressure groups exist to fight for human rights issues and against discrimination, including sexism, racism, and homophobia. **International pressure group:** Amnesty International

11. **Ensuring the rights of children.** As a vulnerable group, children are more likely to be exploited. Some international pressure groups exist specifically to promote and protect the rights of children. **International pressure groups:** the Red Cross and the Red Crescent

12. **Political reform.** Other international pressure groups exist to promote political reform to ensure that there is freedom of speech and that governments do not abuse their powers. **International pressure group:** Human Rights Watch

Rank the 12 examples of international pressure group issues given above in order of importance, starting with the most important and finishing with the least. Share your top three with the rest of the class.

FOR YOUR FILE

Imagine you won £100 to donate to an international pressure group of your choice. Explain which organisation you would give it to and why.

Making a difference?

Getting the message across

Local and national pressure groups use a range of methods to get their message across. These include drawing up petitions, sending mailings, distributing leaflets, running advertising campaigns, and lobbying politicians. They also use the media, e.g. by sending out press releases to gain publicity for events, such as demonstrations.

In order to get their message across, international pressure groups use similar methods to other pressure groups. However, due to the size of the audiences they are trying to influence, they often have bigger, more dramatic campaign techniques.

Protest days

In order to highlight their cause, an international pressure group may hold a special day to draw attention to their issue. An example is International AIDS day, which seeks to draw attention to the suffering of people who are HIV positive or who have AIDS.

One recent problem has been the growing number of pressure groups – locally, nationally, and internationally. As a result, in any given week there are several protest days for different pressure groups. If the public gets swamped with information, this could make pressure groups' messages less effective. However, the strength of organised events is the size, especially when they are co-ordinated internationally. When people all over the world take some action media attention is generated.

Protest days are an effective way to draw attention to issues

Lengthy, co-ordinated campaigns

Because of their size, international pressure groups can also run campaigns that last longer and involve more people. Groups of protesters present in every single city forces people to take notice.

High profile media stunts

Sometimes pressure groups feel that the only way to get attention is to do something outrageous. Such stunts may be expensive, but if they attract enough attention worldwide, it is worth it. An example is in 2003, when Greenpeace launched boats to intercept vessels carrying nuclear waste.

Civil disobedience

Some international pressure groups choose to use illegal action to get their message across. Often, these actions break the law, but do not physically harm anybody. This is known as 'civil disobedience'.

An example of this is when, in dictatorship or in conflict zones, people break the law to gather evidence of human rights abuses. For instance, during the Second Gulf War in 2003–4, peace activists broke through Israeli security in order to gather evidence of alleged atrocities against the Palestinians.

Discuss the views below.

"The ends do not justify the means. You cannot break the law, just to get your point across."

"If no one gets hurt, why shouldn't people make an informed decision to break the law? But they should be willing to accept the punishment that goes with it."

Getting involved

"I joined CAAT (Campaign Against the Arms Trade) because I'm concerned about landmines and the way they kill people and ruin their lives by maiming them, even after a conflict has ended.

I saw this documentary on TV about an African country. The people had all come back to their village but there were lots of places they couldn't go because of land mines.

One day this teenage boy stepped on a mine and it blew his leg off. I support CAAT because they campaign to get the manufacture of landmines banned completely."

Mel

"I decided to support Water Aid for a number of reasons, not only because they want to make sure that people in poorer countries don't have to walk several kilometres to get their water, but also because they aim to provide everyone in the world with clean water.

I read about the diseases that can be caught if all you have to drink is dirty water that's been polluted by sewage. So I decided Water Aid was the pressure group I wanted to join."

Harid

Which international issues concern you the most? Which international pressure group or groups would be your first choice to support?

Volunteering

Case study: working in Africa

When Laura was 18, she volunteered to spend her gap year working in a school in Africa before she trained as a teacher:

"I was very keen to spend a gap year abroad. However, when I applied to do voluntary service in Africa, they told me that my contribution would be much more valuable if I was already a trained teacher. They explained that what was needed most were trained people with the skills they could pass on to local people, rather than unskilled volunteers. So I trained as a teacher and then spent a year in Africa.

Working as a volunteer passes on valuable skills

It was a rewarding, if sometimes harrowing, experience. We take so much for granted in a country such as Britain. In the area where I worked in Africa, the school didn't have the equipment or supplies that we have and the number of people who wanted to learn was overwhelming. But the staff were wonderful and I learned a lot from the students. It's altered my whole way of looking at things."

❶ Discuss what Laura says about why her voluntary service was so rewarding.

❷ Would you ever consider doing voluntary work abroad? If so, what would you like to do? Who would you like to help? Give reasons for your answers.

FOR YOUR FILE

Choose an international issue about which you are concerned. Imagine you work for a pressure group and draft a letter asking people for their support on that issue.

9 DEVELOPING YOUR OWN VALUES

Confronting social and moral issues

Aim: To consider different opinions on social and moral issues, and to explore your own views and opinions (PSHE 1b/Citizenship 2a, 2b, 2c)

Adding value

An important part of anyone's identity is what values they hold. Having values and opinions that are well thought out and deeply felt can give you strength both in yourself and in the world. So where do you stand on the big issues of today?

Teenagers react against 'anything goes' society

Binge-drinking, under-age sex, and misbehaviour are commonly associated with teenagers – but young people are a lot more conservative than their elders might think, according to a survey by *Bliss* magazine. Five thousand teenagers, aged between 12–18, were interviewed. Here are some of the results:

Teenage attitudes

Two-thirds thought there were too many abortions.

Seven out of 10 said cannabis should not be legalised.

One in eight 15-year-olds said having to pay tuition fees would put them off going to university.

Eight out of 10 thought 'bogus' asylum seekers should be sent back.

84% supported harsher sentences for adult criminals.

78% said ID cards should be introduced.

92% believed in marriage.

60% felt it was best for couples to marry before having children.

Patriotism

86% said they were proud to be British.
70% feared Britain's identity would be lost through further European integration.
87% said 'No' to the euro.

Proud to be British?

The monarchy

Two-thirds wanted to keep the royal family and Parliament rather than have a presidential republic, though Prince William was a more popular choice than his father to be king.

Helen Johnston, the editor of *Bliss*, said: "Teenagers like boundaries, they make them feel safe – but over the years they've been torn down… This survey is a damning indictment of the damage caused by the lax attitudes of adults inflicted on children."

FROM AN ARTICLE BY REBECCA ALLISON, *THE GUARDIAN*

1 Are you surprised by any of the results in the survey of teenagers' attitudes?

2 What do you think the editor of *Bliss* means when she says, "Teenagers like boundaries, they make them feel safe – but over the years they've been torn down." Do you agree?

Katie believes in God and marriage. Her mother doesn't.

Katie Lodwidge's life revolves around hair, make-up, shoes and clothes, according to her mother. The 15-year-old reads teenage magazines, talks for hours to her friends, enjoys dancing, singing and aerobics, and hates tidying her bedroom.

But behind this façade of normal teenage behaviour, Katie has developed a keen sense of morality and conservative social attitudes that contrast with the more liberal views of her mother, Alyson Pratt, 38.

Katie believes strongly in marriage and hopes to walk down the aisle one day. She feels that it is all right for people to have children outside marriage if they love each other and are in a stable relationship, but she wants to get married first.

This surprises Alyson, a legal secretary, who says she did not marry Katie's father. "I don't believe in marriage in this day and age because things have changed and so many marriages end in the heartache and nastiness of divorce."

Katie believes in God. Her mother is an atheist. Katie is proud to be British, her mother is stumped by the question. Katie wants Britain to become more integrated with the rest of Europe whereas her mother is firmly against it.

Katie says abortion is a serious step only to be undertaken when there is a good reason. Alyson supports abortion on demand because it is a woman's right to choose.

On drugs, the teenager is against legalisation of cannabis because it will encourage young people to experiment and will fail to stop the dealers who will buy up supplies to sell cut-price on the streets. She wants tougher penalties for drugs. Her mother says cannabis should be legalised. "People are going to get hold of it, whether it is against the law or not."

On tougher penalties for crime their views coincide and both would like to see the death penalty brought back for child killers.

Their views diverge again on whether there should be tougher penalties to discourage under-age sex. Katie thinks there should be, to act as a deterrent. Her mother says tougher sanctions would make no difference. "If they want to have sex they will do it and I blame parents. It's up to parents to educate their children about the dangers of under-age sex, not schools. I know of people who allow their 13- and 14-year-old daughters to entertain boyfriends in their bedrooms. That will never happen in this house!"

"I am surprised by some of my daughter's views. I had no idea she was thinking so deeply about the issues," says Alyson. Katie wants to get back to washing her hair.

FROM AN ARTICLE BY LIZ LIGHTFOOT IN THE *DAILY TELEGRAPH*

---

1 Make a list of the key points in 'Katie believes in God and marriage'.

2 Do you agree that teenagers are often more conservative than their parents?

3 Choose three issues and discuss your own views on them.

Create your own survey using 6–10 of the issues covered in both articles. Think carefully about how you will phrase the questions and then ask the following people to answer your questionnaire:

- Two people your own age
- Two people who are middle aged
- Two people who are over 60.

Do you notice that different age groups have different views? Present your findings in a class discussion.

Aim: To examine two social and moral dilemmas, and explore your own views and opinions (PSHE 1b/Citizenship 2a, 2b, 2c)

Sex before marriage?

Don't touch me there

How do you persuade teenagers there is value in virginity? Joanna Moorhead compares US-style moral pledges with British sex education

For years, school sex education programmes have been criticised for being too liberal: too much about oral sex, too much about homosexual relationships, too much detail, too much everything.

Now, though, we are seeing an about-turn. Next month, six mothers will launch a US-style 'chastity tour' called the Ring Thing, inviting the nation's teenagers to a night of music, lights, fun and drama at which they will buy a silver ring and take a pledge of abstinence until marriage.

And that's not all. Over the past few years, 104 schools throughout the UK have pioneered an education scheme called A PAUSE (Added Power and Understanding in Sex Education). This is a fairly conservative programme aimed at combating the sorts of stereotypical views and behaviours that lead teenagers to think that early sex is something they, and everyone else, has to engage in.

Now a leaked government-backed report has said the programme is working: children, especially girls, who were involved in it, developed a 'more mature' response to sex and were 'less likely to be sexually active' than peers who received traditional forms of teaching.

What do the Ring Thing and A PAUSE have in common? For a start, both are about peer education. "I got involved in the Ring Thing after I saw a TV documentary about it," says Kathi Bellafiore, who has a daughter aged 12 and a son aged 22. "So much of it is done through peers standing up there and giving them a message."

FROM THE GUARDIAN

1 Discuss what you have learned from the article 'Don't touch me there'. Why do you think programmes like the Ring Thing and A PAUSE appear to be working?

2 Do you believe that you should abstain from sexual contact until you are married or in a committed relationship?

1 Discuss the statement below. Do you agree?

> **"The government needs to be telling young people not to have sex yet, rather than telling them sex is fine but they need to be using contraception."**
>
> *Robert Whelan, Director of the Family Education Trust*

2 Do you think abstinence should be taught as part of sex education lessons in schools? Or should sex education consist of giving children frank information about sex and contraception? Give reasons for your views.

Human cloning

Human cells cloned: babies next?

by Roger Highfield and David Derbyshire

South Korean scientists have produced the first convincing evidence that they had cloned a human embryo – a breakthrough that could revolutionise medicine.

The team of researchers created 30 cloned embryos using tissue and eggs donated by women and grew them in a laboratory for 5–6 days. The embryos were then destroyed to produce a potentially unlimited supply of spare part tissue for one of the women. Efforts to clone males using ear tissue from men and tissue from women other than the egg donor were unsuccessful.

Is human cloning a breakthrough?

Scientists described the experiment as an "exciting breakthrough". Scientists said that therapeutic cloning could lead to new treatments for a wide range of ailments, including Alzheimer's, diabetes and heart disease.

Professor Woo Suk Hwang, the head of the privately-funded team, said the development of the two types of cloning – reproductive and therapeutic – could not be separated and called on all countries to outlaw reproductive cloning.

The embryos were not cloned to create babies but were part of wider research into therapeutic cloning. Dr Don Kennedy, the editor-in-chief of *Science*, said, "Nobody has cloned a human here… It is a recipe for cloning only so far as catching a turtle is the recipe for turtle soup. Nobody is going to clone any people with this technique."

Linda Kelly, of the Parkinson's Disease Society, said the experiments were "a milestone in medical research". And Alistair Kent, the director of the Genetic Interest Group, which represents medical charities and support groups, said: "It is good news for patients."

However, religious and pro-life groups condemned the research. Patrick Cusworth of Life, said the scientists had "demonstrated contempt for early human life. To create a new human being with the intention of mutilating and destroying it can never be justified."

Dr Helen Watt, the director of the Catholic Church's Linacre Centre for healthcare ethics, said that therapeutic cloning was morally worse than reproductive cloning, which is illegal in Britain. "Reproductive cloning is bad but it does not have a 100 per cent mortality rate, whereas in therapeutic cloning all the embryos die."

Opponents of therapeutic cloning say there are alternatives that do not use embryos. Research on stem cells found in children and adults suggests that they could be turned into different types of tissue for transplant. However, scientists have had only limited success in that field.

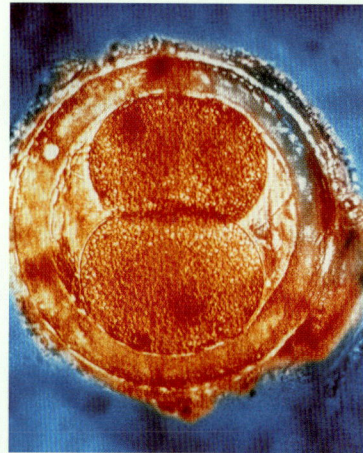

FROM WWW.TELEGRAPH.CO.UK/NEWS

① **Discuss what you have learned about human cloning.**

② **What is the difference between therapeutic cloning and reproductive cloning? Do you think that one will inevitably lead to the other?**

① **Discuss whether you feel the scientific breakthrough of human cloning is a 'breakthrough for patients'. Or do you condemn the research?**

② **Organise a class debate to consider whether human cloning is wrong or right.**

10 MANAGING YOUR TIME AND STUDIES

Coping with revision

Aim: To improve your study skills, especially when revising for exams (PSHE 1a)

Planning ahead

How good are you at managing your time or planning ahead at your studies? So much time is spent preparing for exams and completing course work assignments, that it is important that you structure your time effectively.

Planning will help you break down your work into manageable tasks, and ensure that you don't leave everything to the last minute. Follow the tips (right) if you want to be an expert planner – it's one of the best and easiest ways of making sure your revision is really effective.

Planning your work will ensure you don't leave everything to the last minute

Top tips for successful planning

1. **Set yourself targets.** These give you something to aim for and allow you a sense of achievement when you reach them.

2. **Think about all your goals.** Make sure that your goals are sufficient. They must ensure that you achieve what you want to do.

3. **Be realistic.** If you set yourself targets that you cannot achieve, you will set yourself up for failure and frustration.

4. **Be flexible.** Don't expect that you will be able to keep to your timetable without a hitch. Something is likely to crop up to upset your planning, so be prepared to make some late adjustments.

5. **Don't overplan.** This can be an excuse for not starting important work. If your original targets turn out to be unrealistic, you can always revise your work schedule later.

6. **Monitor your progress.** Check whether you are keeping up with your work schedule. Make any necessary adjustments if you fall behind.

❶ On your own, draw up a study planner for the next month using the advice above.

❷ In pairs, look at each other's monthly study planners and discuss whether you think the goals set down are sufficient, realistic and flexible. Can you suggest ways in which your partner's study plan could be improved?

Learn actively

How do you revise? Do you re-read your notes? Do you learn them by covering up the page and testing yourself?

To help you distinguish the useful from the useless approaches, you need to spot the differences between the following two types of revision:

1. Passive revision – this involves taking information in without attempting to reproduce it in a new way. It will always let you down.

2. Active revision – this involves reproducing what you learn in some way, usually by condensing it. It engages your mind in a creative effort. The more creative, the more memorable. It's the best way to learn.

PASSIVE REVISION

✗ Rereading

Simply reading your notes over and over again doesn't engage the mind. It'll probably make you fall asleep instead. You take the information in, but do nothing with it to fix it in your mind.

✗ Copying out

This has the same problem – and, even worse, it takes forever. You'll find that your brain will be concentrating on getting the words down exactly right, rather than on anything more useful or creative.

✗ Putting your notes on computer

Another waste of time – see above. Why should you need your notes on computer? You're not getting them published.

✗ Highlighting

Highlighting key words and passages takes less time than the passive methods above, but you're only kidding yourself if you think this is a useful activity. It makes your notes look colourful, but does nothing to fix them in your mind.

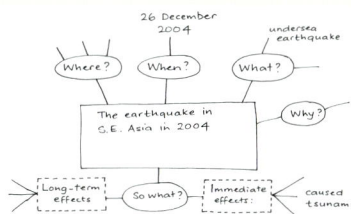

Mind maps help to stimulate the creative side of the brain

ACTIVE REVISION

✓ Writing index cards

Boiling down your material into key points that you can fit on index cards makes you think about what you are reading. It also makes your notes easy to refer back to.

✓ Annotating your texts

Making notes in the margins of your texts is an effort to understand their meaning. You have to work out what the passage is about, and put this into your own words.

✓ Mind mapping

This is a very effective and personal way to reproduce and understand your notes. Because it makes use of colour, drawing and space, mind mapping stimulates the creative side of the brain. It also makes information easy to record and recall.

✓ Repeating out loud

Talking out loud is an excellent method of getting you to think creatively about something. Ask someone to test you, or simply talk to the wall. If you're trying to learn a list of things, repeating or chanting it over and over again really fixes it in your mind (remember doing times tables?).

✓ Doing past papers

When you're ready, try doing a past paper. This will force you to remember everything that you need to know – or show up where you have to do further revision. It also makes you familiar with the way your exam papers are laid out, and the sort of questions that are asked.

FROM *THE STUDENT'S GUIDE TO EXAM SUCCESS* BY EILEEN TRACY

1 Are you an active or a passive reviser? Give reasons.

2 Which methods of revision work best for you? Should you change your approach, and if so, how?

FOR YOUR FILE

Summarise the key points from the information above on active revision. Create a mind map of ways to improve your revision technique.

Coping with exams

Aim: To explore strategies to use when preparing for and taking exams (PSHE 1a)

Beat pre-exam stress

Stress can show up in lots of different ways. Tiredness, change in appetite, aches and pains, sleep problems, itching and rashes, and feeling emotional are just a few. If you're really stressed you might also have panic attacks.

Here are some great tips to help bust stress before an exam:

- Get plenty of sleep, eat a healthy diet and do lots of physical activities.
- Don't spend the whole time locked up with your books. Take regular breaks.
- Try not to feel guilty or anxious when you're not revising. Staying calm will help you remember what you revise and help you to perform better in an exam.
- In the exam you'll feel less stressed the more prepared you are, so start revising as early as you can.

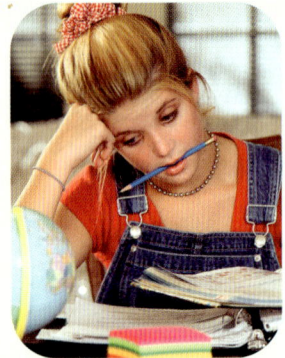

FROM WWW.BBC.CO.UK

1 How do you feel as you approach an exam? Discuss your feelings with other members of the group.

2 Make a list of the points made in the article 'Beat pre-exam stress'. Do you use any other stress-busting methods that you can share with the group?

Exams – your strategy for success

PANIC! This is a common response to the word 'exam'. To cope with this response, it is important to feel in control. You need a strategy.

Eight-point exam strategy

1. When is the exam? (Write it on your year planner.)
2. What kind of exam? (Essay or multichoice.)
3. How long is the exam?
4. How many questions?
5. Do all the questions have to be answered, or is there a choice?
6. How many questions have to be answered from each section?
7. Do all the questions carry an equal number of marks?
8. How long will it take to read the exam paper? (By knowing how long it will take to read, and allowing five minutes for proofreading at the end, you can work out how much time is left and how long you can spend on each question.)

FROM *STUDY SKILLS: A PUPIL'S SURVIVAL GUIDE* BY CHRISTINE OSTLER

Read 'Exams – your strategy for succcess' and 'Exam survival'. Draw up a shortlist of the six most useful points. Be prepared to explain why you have selected those six points.

Exam survival

The day before

1. Check the contents of your pencil case (it must be see-through). Have you a back-up pen, geometry equipment, etc? Do you have fresh batteries in your calculator?
2. Double check the time of the exam and where it will be.
3. Read through your revision notes, but don't work too late.
4. Get some fresh air: don't stay in all day.
5. Have an early night, even if you can't get to sleep straight away.

On the day

1. Get up in plenty of time.
2. Eat some breakfast, even if it is only dry toast!
3. Check that you have everything you need.
4. Get to the place of the exam in plenty of time.
5. Don't talk to students who are over-excited or depressed.
6. Go to the loo.

At the start of the exam

1. Listen to the instructions carefully.
2. Put your watch on the table to keep an eye on the time.
3. Read the instructions carefully.
4. If there is a choice, read all the questions first.
   - Put a ✓ against those you think you could tackle.
   - Put a ✗ against those you definitely couldn't answer.
   - Put a ? against those you are not sure about.
   - Decide which question to answer first. Choose the easiest.
5. If you are stuck and can't find a question you can answer, see if there is one with three or four short sections. You might be able to answer one or two of them, so you will pick up some marks.
6. If you are running out of time and can't get the last answer finished, make sure you have made a plan containing all the important points. You may pick up some extra marks.
7. Try to proofread at the end.

After the exam

If you can avoid it, don't compare answers with your friends.

If you are free, go and do something nice. You deserve it.

FROM *STUDY SKILLS: A PUPIL'S SURVIVAL GUIDE* BY CHRISTINE OSTLER,

FOR YOUR FILE

"I get so stressed by exams that during my mocks I couldn't sleep. And I always run out of time in an exam. What should I do?"

Gus

Write a reply to Gus.

Answer the question!

One of the examiners' most common complaints is that a student hasn't answered the question. Usually this is because the student's answer contains irrelevant material. There are two good ways of avoiding this pitfall:

- **Read the question carefully.**

- **Think about what aspect of the topic the examiner is asking you to write about.**

For example, the exam question is 'Explain the causes of the Black Death'. The phrase 'Black Death' may release a torrent of interesting information, all ready-formed in the memory banks of your brain. However, unless your answer is focused on explaining 'the causes' of the Black Death, much of it will be irrelevant, and you will lose precious marks.

It's also important to look at the instruction words the exam question has used. For example, 'Outline the arguments for and against abortion' will require a different answer from 'Comment on the arguments for and against abortion'. The second question asks you to give your own opinion on the arguments, whereas the first question does not.

The following instruction words often appear in exam questions.
- **Compare and contrast**
- **Evaluate**
- **Analyse**
- **Illustrate**
- **Give an account of...**

Write down what you understand by these phrases and compare your answers with other groups.

11 THINKING AHEAD: PLANNING YOUR FUTURE

Your options at 16

Aim: To examine choices in education, work or training available after the end of Year 11 (PSHE 1f, 1g)

What are your options at 16?

There are lots of options available after Year 11. Do you want to stay on in the sixth form? Or move to a further education college? Do you want to start work as an apprentice? Or even start your own business? You have to make the decision that is right for you. The flowchart below starts you thinking in a broad way about the main choices on offer.

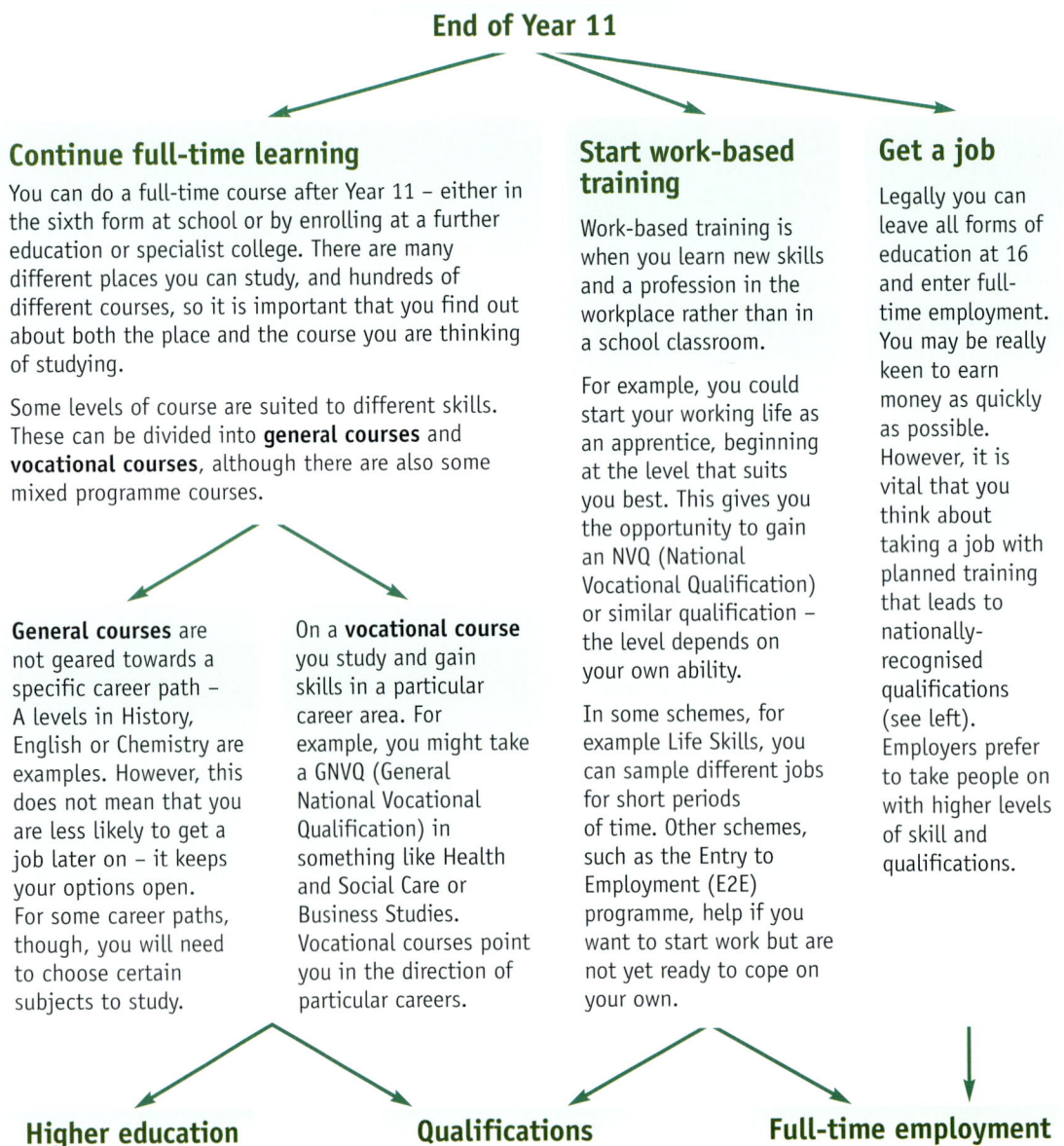

End of Year 11

Continue full-time learning

You can do a full-time course after Year 11 – either in the sixth form at school or by enrolling at a further education or specialist college. There are many different places you can study, and hundreds of different courses, so it is important that you find out about both the place and the course you are thinking of studying.

Some levels of course are suited to different skills. These can be divided into **general courses** and **vocational courses**, although there are also some mixed programme courses.

General courses are not geared towards a specific career path – A levels in History, English or Chemistry are examples. However, this does not mean that you are less likely to get a job later on – it keeps your options open. For some career paths, though, you will need to choose certain subjects to study.

On a **vocational course** you study and gain skills in a particular career area. For example, you might take a GNVQ (General National Vocational Qualification) in something like Health and Social Care or Business Studies. Vocational courses point you in the direction of particular careers.

Start work-based training

Work-based training is when you learn new skills and a profession in the workplace rather than in a school classroom.

For example, you could start your working life as an apprentice, beginning at the level that suits you best. This gives you the opportunity to gain an NVQ (National Vocational Qualification) or similar qualification – the level depends on your own ability.

In some schemes, for example Life Skills, you can sample different jobs for short periods of time. Other schemes, such as the Entry to Employment (E2E) programme, help if you want to start work but are not yet ready to cope on your own.

Get a job

Legally you can leave all forms of education at 16 and enter full-time employment. You may be really keen to earn money as quickly as possible. However, it is vital that you think about taking a job with planned training that leads to nationally-recognised qualifications (see left). Employers prefer to take people on with higher levels of skill and qualifications.

Higher education   **Qualifications**   **Full-time employment**

Case study 1: Michelle

Michelle wants to 'work with money' but has decided to do more full-time learning after her GCSEs before she starts employment in finance. Gaining further qualifications means that she could start at a higher level in her job.

Michelle then had to decide whether to go to college or stay on at school to study.

"I started out by wanting to go to college but then I changed my mind. I talked to my brother and to people I know who have studied at college, to find out more about what it would be like.

"I then decided that I'm the sort of person who would be too distracted by the new social life offered at college and that I should stay on at school with teachers and friends who know me."

Her Year 11 studies include a GNVQ intermediate course in Business Studies, as well as GCSEs. She really enjoys the course work approach and is planning to do an AVCE (Advanced Vocational Certificate of Education) in Business and an A level in Maths.

Case study 2: Brett

As the eldest child in his family, Brett knew that he enjoyed spending time with younger children, but didn't consider childcare as a career idea when he first left school. He started out doing a computer course that he didn't enjoy, and then spent some time working as a security guard. Hearing from a friend about apprenticeships in childcare made him realise that he could train and be paid for something he enjoyed doing.

On his apprenticeship, Brett is working towards NVQ Level 2 in Childcare and Early Years and is hoping to progress onto NVQ Level 3.

"Apprenticeships are a good idea; they are a way of getting qualifications in the workplace rather than sitting in the classroom and being told what to do."

Brett works at a primary school, and while admitting to 'having had a bit of stick for wanting to work with young children', he's glad that he didn't take any notice. His long-term ambition is to become a self-employed childminder.

FROM THE DFES 'IT'S YOUR CHOICE' BOOKLET

1 Discuss what you have learned about some of the different options that are available at the end of Year 11.

2 Draw up a list of advantages for each of the main options given in the flowchart (left): continuing in full-time learning; starting work-based training; and getting a job. What disadvantages are there?

FOR YOUR FILE

1 Write a personal statement describing what choices attract you after Year 11. Give reasons for your statements and don't be afraid to express doubts or uncertainties.

2 "You don't need any qualifications these days." *Jennifer*

Write a reply to Jennifer.

Further education and training

What are the options?

Staying in full-time education

When choosing your further education course, you need to think about whether you prefer exam-based study or coursework and continuous assessment. Look at the course syllabus, and think about your future career plans. What are your predicted GCSE grades? Is your GCSE 'profile' strong enough and broad enough for your chosen course of study?

All schools and colleges publish a free prospectus. This booklet includes information about its facilities and the courses on offer, and should be available in your school's Connexions/careers library or local Connexions resource centre, or call any school or college and ask them to send you one. Try to go along to an open day or evening to check out the place and ask a few questions.

Training and employment

When considering these options you will need to think about what opportunities could develop, and what kind of work you want to do in the future. What skills will you acquire at work? How will the training and experience you get enable you to achieve your ambitions?

Think about what support or supervision is available, as these are opportunities for reviewing your progress. What can you find out about the trainer's or employer's previous experience with school leavers?

Finally, think about how you will cope financially. What will you feel about continuing to live at home if finances make other choices impossible?

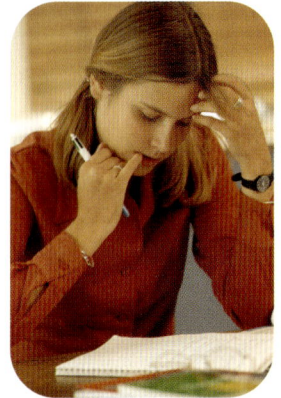

Qualifications at a glance

Level	Type	Academic/general qualifications	Vocational qualifications	Occupational
Entry level	Certification of educational achievement			
1	Foundation (Skills level)	GCSE grades D–G (including applied subjects)	BTEC Introductory Award (First Certificate/Diploma)	NVQ Level 1
2	Intermediate (Good general job skills)	GCSE grades A–C (including applied subjects)	BTEC First Diploma OCR National Certificate	NVQ Level 2 Apprenticeship
3	Advanced (Supervisory/Junior Technician/Craft)	GCSE AS/A levels (including applied subjects)	BTEC National Diploma OCR National Diploma CACHE Diploma	NVQ Level 3 Advanced Apprenticeship
4	Higher (Junior/Middle Management/ Technician)	Degree	Vocational degree, e.g. medicine Foundation degree Higher National Diploma (HND)	NVQ Level 4 and 5

Looking at qualifications in depth

AS/A2 levels

- Advanced levels are on offer in a wide range of general academic or applied subjects.
- Most students take three or four subjects in the first year, and then specialise in their second year by reducing study to two or three subjects.
- An AS level is gained for each subject in which a year of study and exams is successfully completed.
- If a second successful year is completed (known as an A2), a full A level is gained.
- An Advanced Extension Award is available – as well as an A level – in some subjects, to show a greater depth of understanding (see below).
- An AS level is worth three advanced units for entry into higher education.
- An A level (AS + A2) is worth six advanced units for entry into higher education. However points are not counted for an AS pass once the full A level is gained.

Applied AS/A2 levels

- These are on offer in a wide range of vocational subjects.
- Courses develop the knowledge and skills needed for jobs in a broad field of work, for example, hospitality and catering, leisure and tourism, or engineering.
- They can be taken as a single AS (3-unit) award, a double (6-unit) award, a single award (3 AS + 3 A2 units), or a double award (6 AS + 6 A2 units).
- As qualifications for higher education, they are the equivalent of A levels.

Advanced Extension Award (AEA)

- These are currently available in 17 subjects.
- They are designed to stretch the most able A level students – requiring an even greater depth of understanding, logic and critical skills than A levels.

BTEC qualifications

- BTEC stands for the Business and Technology Education Council who award specialised vocational qualifications to people that successfully complete a BTEC course of study. The main courses are:
  - First Certificates (part-time study) and Diplomas (full-time study) for one year. You may need some GCSEs at grades D–G for entry.
  - National Certificates (part-time study) and Diplomas (full-time study), which take two years. Usually four GCSEs at grades A–C are needed for entry, or a BTEC First Diploma or an NVQ Level 2.
  - Higher National Certificate (HNC) and Higher National Diploma (HND) are available in subjects such as business studies, engineering and IT. These are usually taken at age 18+ after getting Advanced or Level 3 qualifications (see chart left).

NVQs

- National Vocational Qualifications (NVQs) relate to real work, testing how competent you are in carrying out the task of a particular job.
- Most people who study for an NVQ are working at the same time.
- The NVQ is directly related to the work you are doing.
- There are NVQs for most jobs and industries.
- You can take NVQ qualifications at five levels (1–5). They are divided up into units, each covering aspects of your job.
- There are no formal entry requirements, although the higher levels need more experience of the work.

FROM IT'S YOUR CHOICE

FOR YOUR FILE

Find a job advert at each level of qualification in the table left. Note down the basic facts about each job, such as the job title and description, skills asked for, qualifications required, and the salary.

Using the information on this spread, and knowledge about yourself (such as your personal strengths, interests and predicted grades), chart two possible routes for your future. You may like to do this in the form of a flowchart.

Applying for jobs

Aim: To understand what makes a good job application form and CV, and how to prepare for an interview (PSHE 1f, 1g)

Job applications

Applying for a job may seem a daunting thing to do, but if you take care over your application, and follow a few simple rules, you will have as good a chance as anyone else. There are three different ways in which you can be asked to present yourself:

1. Application forms

An application form will ask you to give facts about yourself, and to list your experience, activities and interests.

You may be asked to write a paragraph saying why you are applying for that particular vacancy, and what skills you think you can bring to the job.

It's a good idea to use a black pen when filling out the form, and to practise completing a photocopy of the form first.

2. Letters of application

Some employers may ask you to put information about yourself in a letter of application. The key things to remember are to:

- keep the letter short – no more than two sheets of paper
- include your address and phone number
- state the title of the job you are applying for, and where you heard about it
- explain why you are interested in this job, and give details of any related work experience you have done
- give contact details for any referees who have agreed to provide references for you
- write the letter out in rough first and then get someone to check the spelling and grammar.

3. CVs

Most employers will ask you to send a CV when applying for a job. A CV is a brief summary of the important facts about yourself and your experience. You can keep it on your computer and adapt it to send to many prospective employers.

A traditional CV lists, in date order, your education, qualifications and work experience. However, you may want to write a 'skills-based'* CV if you feel your skills are more relevant than your qualifications.

* There is an example of a 'skills-based' CV on page 57, which was sent in reply to a job advert asking for a trainee motor mechanic.

Taking care over a job application could get you an interview

FROM *16 AND BEYOND* © HEREFORD AND WORCESTER CAREERS SERVICE 2001

1 Your teacher will give you a job advert. Discuss how you would write a letter of application.

2 Draft your own letter of application and then comment on your partner's draft, suggesting ways in which they could improve it.

3 Produce a final copy of your letter of application on your own.

FOR YOUR FILE

Write your own CV – it can be either a traditional or a 'skills-based' CV.

Example of a 'skills-based' CV

GRAHAM JONES

22 Lower Grange Road, Dundee, DN4 6HQ
Telephone: 0777 9123687 (mobile)
Date of birth: 13.04.89

Personal skills
● Excellent practical skills, skilled at working with metal and mending things.
● Punctual and reliable.
● Capable and hard worker.
● Good communicator, able to talk to people of all ages.
● Keen to train and gain motor vehicle qualifications.

Education
2002–2005 Dundee City High School.
Predicted to achieve GCSE grades D–E in Technology and Maths.

Work and other relevant experience
● June 2004: in Year 10, did two weeks' work experience placement at Smart Cars Garage, Weston Road, Dundee. Helped the mechanics strip down an engine, replace a gear box and clean up.
● Able to maintain and repair own BMX.

References

Mr H Brake (Manager)
Smart Cars Garage
Weston Road,
Dundee DN4 5BB

Mrs B Temper
Dundee City High School
Cresington Drive
Dundee DN4 8NW

Make it look good:
● Get your CV typed or word-processed. ● Check all the details and spelling. ● Keep it short – two pages at the most.

Preparing for your interview

In your face?

"Aargh! The dreaded interview! What if they don't like me? What if I make a fool of myself?"

Relax! You will be amazed how many people feel like this, particularly when they are inexperienced at interviews. Here are some top tips to help:

● Be polite
● Dress smartly
● Be positive
● Be confident
● Be interested
● Don't be afraid to ask questions
● Do your research – be informed.

Key interview questions

Some questions crop up time and time again in interviews, so it is worth planning your answers to them. Here are some key questions:

"Why do you want to come to this college?"

"Why is this course suitable for you?"

"Tell me about the courses you are doing for school."

"I see from your application form that you are interested in... Tell me something about it."

"What appeals to you about this job?"

"What qualities do you have to offer this company?"

"What do you think are your strengths and weaknesses?"

❶ Read the top tips above and discuss why they are important. What other top tips would you give someone preparing for an interview? Draw up a list of five more tips, then compare them with another pair's list.

❷ Choose a job or college course that you are interested in. Draw up a list of questions that you may be asked and role-play the interviews.

FOR YOUR FILE

Write an advice leaflet on one of the following:
● **writing a job application letter**
● **writing a CV**
● **preparing for an interview.**

12 MANAGING YOUR MONEY

Borrowing and buying on credit

Aim: To explore the world of borrowing, credit and debt, so as to be able to make informed and prudent choices when thinking about borrowing money (PSHE 1e)

Borrowing money

Banks don't let people under 18 years old borrow money, but when you turn 18 you'll be bombarded with offers of credit cards, store cards and loans!

Borrowing means buying now and paying later. When you borrow, you enter into a contract: the lender agrees to give you a lump sum now, and you agree to make regular payments (usually once a month) to pay back the lump sum. What's in it for the lender? They charge you interest on the amount of the loan.

Interest is expressed as an annual percentage rate (APR), which means you pay so much per cent a year in addition to the amount of the loan. For example, if you borrowed £200 at an APR of 15% and agreed to pay it back after a year, you would pay £30 interest as well as the £200 loan.

Paying by credit card, or using your credit card at an ATM, can lead to high interest repayments

Different ways to borrow

Credit cards

Credit cards allow you to buy things now and pay for them later. There is a maximum amount that you can borrow at any one time, known as your 'credit limit'. Each month you receive a statement listing what you owe, and you have to pay off at least a minimum amount. If you pay less than the full amount, you are charged interest on the whole balance.

Overdraft

An overdraft is when you spend more money than you have in your bank account. If you need to go overdrawn, you can arrange an overdraft with your bank. If you have an 'unauthorised overdraft' (i.e. running up an overdraft without your bank agreeing to it), the bank could refuse to pay for the cheques that you write.

Bank loan

If you want to borrow a large amount over a period of time, say to pay for a car or stereo system, you could ask a bank to lend you a lump sum. You usually agree to make a fixed payment each month for a set number of years. There's often a charge if you pay off the balance early.

Hire purchase

This is an agreement to pay for goods in instalments. For example, instead of buying a stereo system outright for £500, you could pay 18 monthly payments of £50. Ultimately your stereo will have cost you £900 and you are technically only hiring the goods until you have paid off the final instalment. Store cards work in a similar way.

Method of borrowing	Advantages	Disadvantages
Credit cards	A good way of getting an interest-free loan if you pay off the outstanding balance each month.	An expensive way of borrowing in the long term if you are only able to pay off a small amount of what you owe each month.
Overdraft	Can be a cheap, flexible way to help with temporary cash flow problems: some accounts even allow you to go overdrawn a small amount without paying fees and interest.	An expensive way of borrowing if it's not arranged with the bank in advance. Not suitable for long-term borrowing.
Bank loan	A good way of paying for long-term borrowing, as it allows you to plan your finances.	Not very flexible and watch out for the interest rates on the loan!
Hire purchase	Allows you to pay off a purchase over a long period of time in a planned way.	An expensive way of borrowing, and you don't own the goods until you have paid off the whole loan.

Borrowing tips

1. Only borrow if you really need the item or service and you've worked out how you will repay the money.
2. Don't ignore loan repayments or credit card bills just because you can't afford to pay them. This will make your debt even worse.
3. If your debts are out of hand, get help immediately. See your bank or the Citizens Advice Bureau.
4. Avoid all debt problems by developing your budgeting skills.

Discuss what you have learned on these pages. Draw up a four-question quiz to test your partner.

'Avoid credit card debt', students warned

Consumer rights campaigners today warned students to avoid being seduced into applying for a credit card because of 'gimmicks' such as free cameras and book tokens.

"Taking on credit card debt could push today's already indebted students over the edge," said Mr Mayo, chief executive of the National Consumer Council (NCC). "These free gifts are nothing but seductive offers to be ignored."

Tim, a computer science student at Aston University, said: "When I arrived at my freshers' fair last year, we were all pressed by Barclaycard into applying for credit cards with the offer of free cameras or popcorn makers. I got the popcorn maker but, lucky for me, I decided the card was too risky so I cut it up. I would advise other students to do the same."

A spokesman for Barclaycard accused the NCC of insulting students' intelligence. "We would never go in there and sell credit cards purely on the back of free cameras or other incentives, but the fact is that people like and appreciate these incentives," he said.

FROM WWW.MONEY.GUARDIAN.CO.UK

Plan a radio phone-in programme called 'Money box'. The theme is borrowing money. You must be prepared for different young people to phone in with their questions. One of you is the presenter and the rest are experts on the panel (who can double as questioners). Be prepared to present a programme in front of the class and to receive questions from the 'studio audience'.

FOR YOUR FILE

"I'm about to go to college for three years. I keep getting letters offering me credit cards and I'm quite tempted, especially by the ones that offer free gifts. What should I do?"

Trefor, 18

Draft a reply to Trefor.

Work and pay

Aim: To understand the financial aspects of starting work (PSHE 1e)

How do I get paid?

Whether you are doing a part-time job in a shop or your first full-time job after leaving school, you will find there are various ways in which you may be paid for your work (see right).

How you may be paid	
Wage	Money that is paid daily, weekly, or monthly for work done. There is a national minimum wage (see 'Rates of pay' on the right) that employers must pay to their employees (workers).
Salary	A whole year's pay (usually paid monthly).
Overtime	Money paid for working more hours than in your contract. This is often paid at a higher rate.
Commission	Money paid for work done, either instead of a wage or in addition to a wage. Someone selling gym equipment may get £200 per week plus a commission of 3% of the price of all her sales that week.

Your payslip

National Insurance number: everyone gets a National Insurance (NI) number when they are 16. It is used for identification for work and training, or when claiming benefits.

Income tax: a percentage of your earnings goes to the Inland Revenue (the government) to pay for education, transport, etc. If you are a single person, the first £4745 of your salary is free of tax.

Gross pay: your total monthly pay before any deductions (see right).

Pension scheme contribution: NI contributions only fund a small state pension, so many people decide to put some money aside each month into a separate pension scheme, which may be offered by your employer. The amount would be shown here.

National Insurance (NI) contribution: a percentage of your earnings helps to pay for government social services, such as health and state pensions. What you pay is used to calculate the amount of pension you will receive when you retire.

Net pay: the total amount of pay you take home after all the deductions have been taken out.

MIDCHESTER COUNTY COUNCIL

PAY ADVICE: MR BILL PAYER

EMPLOYEE NUMBER: 115847
NI NUMBER: HD 42 45 62 H
TAX CODE: 474L

DATE: 31.05.05
TAX MONTH: 2

DESCRIPTION	GROSS	DEDUCTIONS		NET PAY
SALARY	750	TAX	57.82	
		NI	38.94	
		PENSION	10.00	
TOTALS	750		106.76	643.24

YEAR TO DATE
GROSS SALARY	1500.00
TAX	115.64
NI	77.88
PENSION	20.00

FROM *STARTING WORK*, CITIZENSHIP FOUNDATION

"I don't agree with paying tax and National Insurance on my earnings. I think people should take home every penny that they earn."

Discuss the statement on the left. Do you agree with it? Give reasons for your views.

The ins and outs of part-time jobs by Carla Neeson

Unless you are 16 years-old and have a National Insurance number, you are not legally allowed to work in a night-time job, or for more than a few hours per day.

A limit of 48 hours per week is set for 16- to 18-year-olds. It is possible to work longer if you want to, but you must sign an 'opt-out' form with your employer. You are also entitled to one day off per week, and to take a break if working a shift of more than six hours. Under-18s cannot work for more than eight hours per day – which is definitely to your benefit!

When it comes down to wages, under-18s are less fortunate as the minimum wage is only £3 per hour. However, think yourself lucky – before October 2004 there was no minimum wage at all for 16- to 17-year-olds!

FROM WWW.TEENZONE.MONSTER.CO.UK

Rates of pay

Recent research carried out by the Abbey bank showed that the average rates of pay for some part-time jobs typically done by young people are:

Chambermaid/hotel cleaner	£4–£6 an hour
Chip shop	£1.20 an hour
Cinema usher	£5 an hour
Department store	£3.55 an hour
Fast-food burger bar	£3.60 an hour
Hairdressing	£1.80 an hour
Paper round	£7 a week
Pizza delivery	£3.20 an hour
Supermarket	£4.50 an hour
Waiter/waitressing	£2–£5 an hour

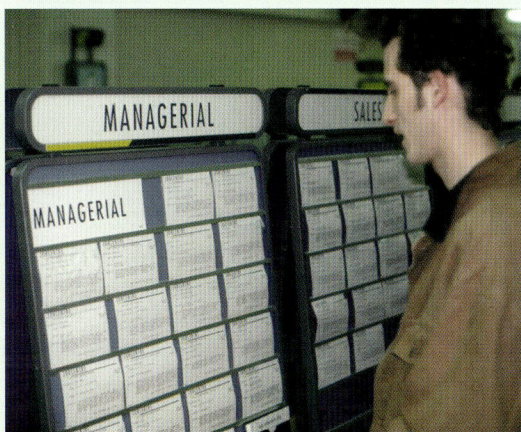

The national minimum wage for workers aged 22 or more is £4.85 per hour; for 18- to 21-year-olds it is £4.10 per hour; for 16- to 17-year-olds it is £3 per hour.

FROM WWW.BBC.CO.UK/RADIO1/ONELIFE/FINANCE

1 **Make a list of jobs that you have already done, or that your brothers and sisters have done. How much do you/they earn? How close is this to the minimum wage? How long do you/they work for? Discuss your findings with the class.**

2 **Do you agree with the national minimum wage? Do you think it is fair for young people?**

Look at some job adverts in your local paper and find out about how they are paid. You may need to telephone the employers to get information on whether overtime or commission is available, and how much and how often an employee is paid.

Draft a reply to Christine.

13 MANAGING STRESS AND DEALING WITH DEPRESSION

Stress

Aim: To understand what stress is and what causes it, and to explore ways of dealing with stress (PSHE 2c)

What is stress? Erica Stewart explains

Anxiety is a feeling of uneasiness or tension about what will happen in the future. It is something that everyone experiences and it's quite normal to feel anxious from time to time.

The teenage years are years of change and it is only natural that you should feel apprehensive about some of the new situations that you have to face. As you grow up, you are expected to take more control of your own life and to make your own decisions. You have to start thinking about what career path you are going to take and cope with the pressures of preparing for important exams.

Your relationships with other members of your family change. You may develop a close relationship with a boyfriend or girlfriend and you have to learn how to handle the strong emotions that this involves. There may be pressures from other friends, too, for example to take risks you are unsure you want to take.

All these things can make you feel anxious. A certain amount of anxiety is good for you. If you didn't worry about doing something risky, you might do something you will later regret. If you didn't feel anxious about passing your exams, you might not bother to do enough revision.

But too much anxiety can make you ill. When you get over-anxious you are said to be suffering from 'stress'.

Some teenagers get stressed because the everyday pressures of coping with life at home and/or at school get on top of them. Others may develop stress because of a life-changing event, such as the death of someone, parents separating or divorcing, or moving to a different area to live.

What stresses you out?

> "I got stressed out when my parents were splitting up. The atmosphere in the house was terrible." *Xavier*

> "My mum keeps on criticising me. She always wants to know what I'm doing." *Jade*

> "I get really wound up about my schoolwork. I used to cope with it, but there seems so much of it now. I worry so much that I can't seem to get started." *Dom*

❶ Discuss the different reasons these teenagers give for feeling stressed.

> "My friends put pressure on me to do things I don't really want to do. I worry that they'll exclude me from the group if I don't join in." *Taz*

❷ What other things cause teenagers stress? Make a list of what you think are the top five causes of stress for teenagers.

> "My boyfriend puts pressure on me. He doesn't understand that I need space and time on my own." *Astrid*

❸ Compare your lists in a class discussion. Discuss whether the causes of stress for boys are different from the causes of stress for girls.

> "I'm anxious about my appearance. I worry that no one will ever find me attractive." *Cal*

Dealing with stress

If you think you are under stress, do two things straight away. Talk to somebody about your problems and put some time into each day to relax. You need to feel that you are in charge of your life. You may need to accept that there are some things you are not able to do. Sort out what's most important and make decisions.

People don't all deal with stress equally well. People who are generally confident and feel they can cope with life's problems will certainly manage better than people who feel helpless. So if you can convince yourself that the problem is not as great as it seems, you'll manage better. Positive thinking really does help.

When you're worried and under stress, it helps a lot if your friends and family are supportive. This works in reverse too. If someone you know is under stress, you can help by showing that person you really care. That's the most important kind of support there is.

FROM *GROWING UP* BY MERLION PUBLISHING

Advice for beating the blues

Get regular exercise. Physical exercise is good for the mind as well as for the body. Studies show that if you exercise regularly, your body creates more beta endorphins (natural hormones that make you feel better about yourself). Also, if you are physically tired you will sleep well.

Exercise can help with depression

Don't hold things in. Have a good cry if you can and talk to anyone who'll listen sympathetically.

Make a list of all the things you really enjoy in life and try to do some of them.

Give yourself something to look forward to every day – like visiting a good friend, watching a favourite video, or buying a magazine.

FROM *GROWING UP* BY MERLION PUBLISHING

1 Study the two articles above on how to deal with stress. Draw two columns. In one column list each piece of advice about how to deal with stress. In the other column list the reasons for the advice.

2 What do you think are the most important pieces of advice in the two articles?

FOR YOUR FILE

You receive a letter from a friend who has moved to another school. She's feeling stressed out. Draft a reply to her suggesting some things she might do to try to relieve her stress.

Depression

Aim: To explore what depression is and different types of depression, and to examine ways of coping with depression (PSHE 2c)

What is depression?

Depression is one of the most common but misunderstood medical conditions. It is estimated that one in four people will suffer from depression at some point in their lifetime.

People who suffer from depression usually experience persistent sadness with feelings of helplessness and hopelessness. These feelings may make it difficult to carry out normal daily activities.

Depression is a condition with a wide range of physical and psychological symptoms, which sometimes make it hard to recognise and understand. Depression can affect anyone and does not reduce your value as a human being.

It is important to remember that:

- Depression is a condition that can affect anyone at any age.
- It is not connected with, and does not develop into, insanity.
- Depression can be treated.
- There is no need to cope alone.

FROM *THE YOUNG PERSON'S GUIDE TO STRESS,* DEPRESSION ALLIANCE

1 Write down 10 things you have learned about depression.

2 Compare your lists in a group or class discussion.

Types of depression

Reactive depression

This is triggered by a traumatic, difficult or stressful event, and people affected will feel low, anxious, irritable, and even angry. Reactive depression can also follow a prolonged period of stress and can begin even after the stress is over.

Endogenous depression

This is not always triggered by an upsetting or stressful event. Those affected by this common form of depression will experience physical symptoms such as weight change, tiredness, sleeping problems and low mood, as well as poor concentration and low self-esteem.

Manic depression (bipolar depression)

People with manic depression experience mood swings, with 'highs' of excessive energy and elation, to 'lows' of utter despair and lethargy. Delusions or hallucinations can also occur. Most people with this condition have their first episode in their late teens or early twenties.

Seasonal Affective Disorder (SAD)

This type of depression generally coincides with the approach of winter. It is often linked to shortening of daylight hours and a lack of sunlight. Symptoms will include wanting to sleep excessively and cravings for carbohydrates or sweet foods. Special 'light boxes' can be used to treat this kind of depression (see right).

Post-natal depression

Many new mothers will experience 'baby blues', such as mood swings, crying spells and feelings of loneliness, three or four days after giving birth. Post-natal depression lasts for much longer and includes symptoms such as panic attacks, sleeping difficulties, having overwhelming fears about dying, and feelings of being unable to cope.

FROM *EVERYTHING YOU NEED TO KNOW ABOUT DEPRESSION,* DEPRESSION ALLIANCE

Coping with depression

Erica Stewart offers advice on things you can do if you're depressed, which can help to lift your mood.

- Do something relaxing. Have a bath, play your favourite music, read a book or magazine.
- Get active. Exercise lessens stress, so go for a walk or a bicycle ride, do some dancing or kick a ball around in the park.
- Eat healthily. Your diet can affect your mood, so try and eat regular meals and make sure you get enough of healthy foods, such as fresh fruit and vegetables.
- Express your feelings. Write about them in a diary or journal, or write a song or a poem. Putting your feelings into words can help you to understand them.
- Share your feelings. Talking to someone about how you feel can help you to understand more clearly what is making you depressed.

TALK TO SOMEONE

"I didn't think I could talk to anyone I knew. I thought it would just make things worse. I couldn't talk to my friends about it because I didn't think they would take it seriously. I felt just completely alone. I wrote to a problem page and they encouraged me to phone a helpline. Once I did that they helped me to have the confidence to get help."

YoungMinds, the children's mental health charity, offers the following advice:

Talking to someone might help you feel more able to cope. Try and talk to someone you like and trust. This might be one of the following:

friend
brother or sister
grandparent
parent or carer
aunt or uncle
friend's parent.

Other people you could talk to may include:

teacher
school counsellor
social worker
school nurse
youth worker.

You can find out about places where young people can go for help: call Youth Access on 020 8772 9900 (Mon–Fri, 9am–5pm), or email: admin@youthaccess.org.uk

Ways to help a friend if they're unhappy or feeling depressed

- Listen and try to be sympathetic.
- Don't expect them to just snap out of it.
- Don't criticise or tease them.
- Try and get them to talk about how they feel.
- Be patient and allow them time to talk.
- Try and help them look for help.

FROM *DO YOU EVER FEEL DEPRESSED?* BY YOUNGMINDS

❶ Discuss things you can do to help yourself if you are suffering from depression.

❷ List the people you can talk to if you are depressed. Who do you think would be the best person to speak to?

❸ Discuss how you can help a friend who is depressed. Make a list of what you would do.

Use the internet to find out more about depression among teenagers and how to deal with it. Useful websites include: www.depressionalliance.org and www.youngminds.org.uk.

14 SAFER SEX

Sexually transmitted infections (STIs)

Aim: To understand what sexually transmitted infections are and how to protect yourself against them (PSHE 2a, 2b, 2e, 2f, 3b)

Be smart, be protected

More than 200 people a day are infected with chlamydia in the UK. Know the facts so you don't put yourself, or others, at risk…

If you're having sex you're at risk of catching an STI, which are caused by germs that can be passed on during sexual contact. Some STIs make you feel uncomfortable, others, like HIV (the virus that causes AIDS) can be life threatening. When used properly, condoms give a great deal of protection against most STIs, including HIV, chlamydia and gonorrhoea, but they aren't a 100% guarantee against genital warts or herpes.

How can I avoid catching an STI?

- Always use condoms for any type of sexual contact, including oral sex.
- Make sure the condom goes on before any contact between the penis and your body.
- Make sure you and your boyfriend know how to put a condom on.
- Say 'NO' to sex with any partner who doesn't want to use a condom – no excuses.
- Don't have sex until you're absolutely 100% sure that you want to.

The most common STIs are:

Chlamydia

Symptoms include: creamy discharge from the penis or vagina; bleeding between sex; irregular periods; pain during sex or when urinating. 70% of girls and 50% of boys don't show any symptoms of this infection. Untreated, it can lead to pelvic inflammatory disease and infertility.

Genital warts

Symptoms include: itchy (not painful) lumps or bumps on the skin anywhere in the genital area.

Gonorrhoea

Symptoms include: yellow or green discharge from the penis, vagina or bottom; bleeding and spotting after sex or between periods; pain when passing urine or during sex.

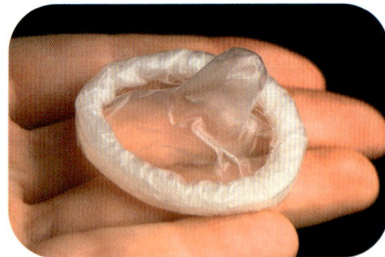

Condoms give protection against most STIs when used properly

Genital herpes

Symptoms include: painful blisters on the skin anywhere in the genital area; swollen glands in the groin; fever; feeling unwell; pain passing urine or during sex.

Syphilis

Symptoms include: ulcers in the genital area or mouth; a rash may appear on the body and hands. If treated, will heal in a few weeks. Untreated, syphilis can lead to problems with hearing, heart or nervous system.

Write down what you have learned about STIs. How are they caught? How can you avoid catching them? How can you tell whether you have an STI?

Real life

Becky, 17, tells how she coped when she discovered she'd caught an STI

"Last summer I met a lad called Tim. We'd been seeing each other for a month when we started sleeping together. At first we used condoms because I was worried about getting pregnant, but when he said sex would be better without them I went on the Pill and stopped using condoms. Things were great until Tim got some bad news.

Tim's ex-girlfriend had contacted him to say she'd caught an STI – chlamydia – so he went for a test and discovered he had it, too. I knew he may have passed it on to me. I told him I never wanted to see him again.

The next morning I went to see the doctor who told me chlamydia is a common STI and that often there are no symptoms. I gave a urine sample and had to wait a week for the results.

When I went back, the doctor told me the test was positive and I burst into tears. The doctor was great and said it was unlikely to cause any long-term damage. She prescribed antibiotics and the chlamydia cleared up.

Now I always use a condom and make sure my boyfriend has been tested for STIs before I get serious with him. If a boy tries to convince you to have sex without a condom, don't do it! Wearing a condom is a lot better than what I had to go through."

FROM *J17*

Discuss Becky's experience. Was she just unlucky and what has she learned?

Before you do it, talk about it

Erica Stewart says, Talk first, then decide whether or not to have sex

The questions you need to ask your partner are:

- How many previous partners have you had?
- Did you ever have unsafe sex with any of them?
- Have you ever had an STI or been tested for one?
- What precautions are we going to take against catching an STI from one another?
- Do you intend to sleep with anyone else during our relationship?

If you can't have such a discussion about your relationship, or do not trust your partner to answer truthfully, then you need to ask yourself: Does this person really care about me? Do I really want to have sex with a person who can't talk about such important things? Is it worth the risk?

What does safer sex involve?

Safer sex involves:

- Using contraception to prevent an unplanned pregnancy.
- Using protection to reduce the risk of catching an STI.
- Abstaining from sexual activities that might put you at serious risk of infection.
- Knowing your partner's sexual history before you have sex together, so that you can make an informed choice about whether or not to have sex with them.

Discuss the statements below and say why you agree or disagree with them.

"Teenagers must learn to be selective about their sexual partners if they want to avoid catching an STI."
Health expert

"It's ridiculous to suggest you should quiz your partner before you have sex. Do you really think they'll give honest answers?"
17-year-old girl

"What's the big deal? If I get an STI, I'll get it treated."
19-year-old boy

"I don't intend to have sex before I'm married. It's common sense to wait – for health reasons as well as moral reasons."
18-year-old girl

FOR YOUR FILE

Imagine you have been asked by the Health Protection Agency to design a poster to warn young people about the risks of STIs. What messages do you want to put across?

HIV and AIDS

Aim: To explore what the facts are about HIV and AIDS, and to examine attitudes to AIDS (PSHE 2a, 2b, 2e, 2f, 3b)

HIV and AIDS: your questions answered

What are HIV and AIDS?

HIV stands for the Human Immunodeficency Virus, which damages the immune system that protects the body from infection. It is sometimes called the AIDS virus, because it is the virus that can lead to the development of AIDS.

AIDS stands for Acquired Immune Deficiency Syndrome. People who have AIDS pick up infections more easily, because the body's protection system has been destroyed. These infections can cause death.

How can you get infected with HIV?

The HIV virus is present in an infected person's bodily fluids – their blood, and their semen or vaginal fluids. The main ways of transmission are:

- through unprotected sexual intercourse
- sharing needles or syringes if you are a drug user.

Other possible ways of infection include:

- getting tattooed or pierced by someone who hadn't sterilised their equipment after using it on an infected person
- sharing a razor with an infected person.

In the past, some people were infected as a result of receiving blood transfusions of infected blood, but blood in many countries is now tested to make sure it doesn't carry the virus.

How can you protect yourself from getting infected?

At present, there is no vaccine that protects against HIV. The way to protect yourself is to practise safe sex.

- Always use a condom when having vaginal, anal or oral sex.
- Discuss your partner's previous sexual experiences with them before consenting to sex.
- Don't be pressurised into having unprotected sex.

Who is most at risk from HIV?

Anyone who practises unsafe sex. Most people who become infected do so as a result of sex between men and women. However in the developed world, certain groups are more at risk. These include:

- homosexual and bisexual men
- intravenous drug users
- people who have been sexually active in countries where HIV is widespread
- anyone who has sex with someone from these high-risk groups.

How can you tell if you're infected?

There are no immediate symptoms. The only way to find out is by having a blood test. But it takes three to six months for the virus to be detectable in the body. You can get advice about having a test from your local Genito-Urinary Medicine (GUM) clinic.

What happens if you become infected?

Most people who are HIV-positive will develop health problems, but it can take 10 or more years for AIDS to develop. However, even though they don't show any signs of illness, they are still infected and can pass on the infection to others.

Can AIDS be cured?

At present, there is no cure for AIDS, but there are drugs that you can take which often manage to slow down the speed at which it develops.

Myths about HIV infection

You won't get HIV:

- by drinking from a glass or eating from a plate that's been used by a HIV-positive person.
- from hugging or shaking hands with someone who is HIV-positive.
- if someone sneezes; the virus doesn't travel through the air.
- if you're bitten by an infected insect, or if you donate blood at a blood transfusion unit.

FROM *SEX ED* BY DR MIRIAM STOPPARD

Draw up a quiz consisting of statements about HIV and AIDS, some of which are 'True' and some of which are 'False'. Join up with another pair and answer each other's quiz.

Ellen's story

Ellen discovered she was HIV positive when she was 16. She went for a test when she found out her boyfriend's previous girlfriend was a drug user and had developed AIDS.

"I didn't expect the test to be positive," she remembers. "When it was, it felt like being given a death sentence. For months, I was just numb, I couldn't take it in."

Now, three years on, she is at college and enjoying life. She has recently started taking a combination of drugs to keep the HIV under control. "I'm on 24 pills a day, and they've all got to be taken at the right times. It's hard to get used to, and sometimes they make me feel really sick. But I know they're my best hope. I try not to think about the future too much; I just concentrate on today and try to get as much out of life as I can."

FROM *SEXUALLY TRANSMITTED DISEASES* BY JO WHELAN

More unsafe sex sends HIV cases soaring

New HIV infections increased by 20% between 2002 and 2003, and are expected to rise to more than 7000, the highest yearly total.

"Increases in unsafe sex are undoubtedly the main driving force behind this epidemic," said Dr Brian Evans of the Health Protection Agency.

"HIV is an infection that is here to stay," Dr Evans said. "With almost a third of the 49 500 people currently living with HIV in the UK still unaware they are infected, the rising trend in new diagnoses is liable to get worse before it gets better."

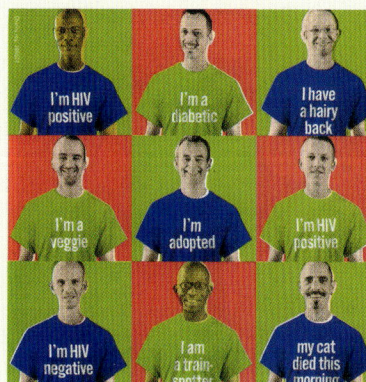

How much would you tell on a first date?
No-one tells everything about themselves, especially to someone they want to have sex with. You choose what to tell, because you can never be sure of the reaction. It isn't always easy to be open about HIV, even after seeing someone for a while. Though it can be a good thing, not everyone tells their HIV status, for all kinds of reasons. Whatever your own views, remember it isn't a duty to tell, it's not a right to be told.

terrence HIGGINS TRUST

Posters and leaflets help to raise awareness of HIV

FROM *THE DAILY TELEGRAPH,* 13 FEBRUARY 2004

❶ What do you learn from Ellen's story about what life is like for someone who is HIV positive?

❷ Discuss why you think the number of HIV infections in Britain are increasing.

Imagine you are part of a government team with the task of organising a campaign to educate young people about the dangers of unsafe sex. How would you get your message across? Discuss ideas for a campaign and draw up a proposal to share with the rest of the class.

Attitudes to AIDS

Read the statements below. What is your attitude to HIV and AIDS? Decide which of the views you most agree with. Share your thoughts in a class discussion.

"AIDS concerns me, so I'm going to make sure I always have sex using a condom and avoid high-risk activities."

"I'm worried sick about catching the HIV virus. I'd rather not have sex than take the risk of catching it and developing AIDS."

"AIDS is like any other disease you might catch. Life's a lottery. The thought I might get AIDS isn't going to stop me from having sex with whoever I fancy."

15 DRUGS AND DRUGTAKING

Drugs: the risks

Aim: To explore the reasons why young people take drugs, to examine the risks, and to provide information about ecstasy (PSHE 2a, 2b, 2e)

Why do young people take drugs?

"I started smoking spliffs when I met my boyfriend Jason. He's three years older than me and he was really into it. I thought I'd look young if I didn't join in."

Natasha, aged 15

"I take speed when I go out 'cos it gives me more energy and I find it easier to chat up girls. It makes me more confident. It's pretty rank the next day though – I feel really tired and depressed."

Matt, aged 18

Let's face it – drugs are a fact of life. At some stage you or one of your mates are going to be offered something. Yeah, loads of drugs are illegal and you're not meant to take them – but at the end of the day the only person who can make those decisions about your lifestyle is you.

The important thing is that when you make those choices you know what you're doing and what's involved.

FROM *TELL IT LIKE IT IS* BY KATIE MASTERS

So what's the deal?

A danger with all drugs is that you never know what effect a drug is going to have on you. Even if it's a drug you've taken before, your body can still react badly to it. That might mean you feel sick or you scare yourself by having weird hallucinations, or, in the worst cases, people can end up dying. Don't think that just because your mates have tried it and they've been all right, that you'll be OK, too. There's no way of knowing what the drug's going to do to you.

Another danger is that when you're given a drug, you don't really know what's in it. Some dealers try and make a profit by adding cheaper ingredients into the drug. So they'll tell you they're selling ecstasy – and what you get is ecstasy mixed up with something else.

Finally, there are the dangers involved in getting the drugs into your body. Injecting drugs is the most dangerous way of taking them. If people share their injecting equipment, they run the risk of contracting blood diseases like HIV or hepatitis. Also, the user doesn't know how much of the drug is going in and that means they're more likely to overdose. If they miss the vein when they inject, they can end up with abscesses and gangrene.

FROM *TELL IT LIKE IT IS* BY KATIE MASTERS

❶ **What do you consider to be the main risks involved in drugtaking?**

❷ **Discuss how young people obtain drugs. What is your attitude towards people who sell drugs to young people?**

What young people say

"I was curious about their effect."

"Drugs are cheap and easily available."

"My friends use them."

"I'm bored."

"I wanted to appear grown up."

"I wanted to rebel."

"I enjoy the buzz they give."

"Drugs helped me escape from personal problems."

"They help me to relax."

"Drugs make me feel more confident."

"I wanted to show off."

Can you think of any other reasons why young people take drugs? Make a list and put the reasons in order of importance, starting with what you think is the main reason. Compare your views in a group discussion.

10 things you need to know about ecstasy

1. Taking ecstasy (or Es) is a gamble. Many tablets are not pure ecstasy. They may not even be Es at all.

2. Because you never know what's in a tablet, you may get a negative reaction to whatever the ingredients are.

3. It can take an ecstasy tablet between 20 minutes and an hour to kick in. Some people have taken another tablet thinking the first one hasn't worked and have given themselves a double dose.

4. You don't know how ecstasy will affect you personally. The drug seems to make people both calm and energetic, but it can cause anxiety, panic attacks and confusion.

5. Ecstasy affects your body's temperature control. If you dance for long periods without stopping regularly to chill out, you run the risk of overheating and dehydration (losing too much body fluid). Users are advised to sip no more than a pint of water or non-alcoholic drink every hour.

6. Drinking too large a quantity of fluids after taking ecstasy can be very dangerous. Ecstasy releases a hormone that stops the production of urine. Drinking a few pints of liquid in a short period will interfere with the salt balance in your body and can be fatal.

7. The comedown from taking ecstasy (the 'ecstasy blues') can leave you feeling tired and depressed.

Clubbers taking ecstasy can run the risk of dehydration

8. No one is sure what the long-term effects are. There is some evidence that ecstasy use may cause brain damage with sustained memory loss and an increased risk of depression. Use of ecstasy has also been linked to liver and kidney problems.

9. Since 1996 over 200 people have died from taking ecstasy.

10. Ecstasy is a class A drug which it is illegal to possess, give away or sell.

Ecstasy kills boy who made anti-drug film

A schoolboy who wrote and directed an anti-drugs film died after taking ecstasy "because he heard it was a laugh".

Ben Henessy, 15, lost consciousness after 'bombing' up to four and a half ecstasy tablets with a friend, only a week after the film was first screened.

The inquest was told Ben had a temperature of 42°C, compared with a normal body temperature of 37°C, when he arrived at hospital.

His internal organs were unable to cope and he began suffering fits and heart failure. Doctors were unable to save him and he died from cardio-respiratory arrest.

FROM *THE DAILY TELEGRAPH*

Discuss why you think people take ecstasy. What do you consider to be the main risk?

FOR YOUR FILE

"What are the risks from taking ecstasy?" *Treena*

Use the information on this page to draft a reply to Treena.

Drugs and the law

Aim: To discuss the drugs laws and to debate whether they should be changed (PSHE 2a, 2b, 2e)

Drug laws: time for a change?

Drug laws were introduced to protect people from harming themselves by taking substances that:

- are dangerous to their health
- might alter their behaviour by making them do odd things
- they might become addicted to.

The Misuse of Drugs Act 1971 prohibits the non-medical use of certain drugs. Drugs are classified according to how dangerous they are considered to be.

Class A drugs include heroin, cocaine, ecstasy, LSD and magic mushrooms.

Class B drugs include speed.

Class C drugs include cannabis and tranquillizers.

It is illegal to possess, supply or manufacture these drugs and punishments range from up to two years and a fine for possession of Class C drugs, to a maximum penalty of life imprisonment and a fine for supplying Class A drugs.

Some people argue that the drug laws are unnecessarily harsh and old fashioned and should be repealed. They advocate legalising all drugs on the grounds that individuals should have the right to decide for themselves whether or not to take substances that might damage their health or endanger their lives, provided that they do not harm or endanger the lives of other people.

Drug facts

- In Britain, 4 million people a year use one or more illegal drugs.
- 250 000 people are described as problematic drug users by the Home Office.
- The social and economic costs of drugs are estimated at £18 billion a year.
- The government spends £1.5 billion a year trying to tackle drugs problems through education, law enforcement and rehabilitation.

❶ Discuss why you think there are drugs laws.

❷ Discuss the views below. Do you think the drugs laws are out of date and need changing?

In my opinion

"Drug addiction causes misery and ruins lives. I should know. I watched my sister's future disappear. Within two years of starting on drugs she was dead from an overdose. To legalise them would be a disaster. We need to catch the dealers, lock them up and throw away the key."

21-year-old brother of a drug victim

"Every time the government hits down on the supply side, it just drives the price up and so crime increases. Our policy so far has been a disaster. We have gone from 5000 heroin users in 1971 to 250 000 now. The only answer is to legalise drugs and reduce demand through education. Cannabis could be sold through off licences, and ecstasy and cocaine could be bought from pharmacists."

Campaigner for reform of drugs laws

"Drugs are far too dangerous to make them freely available. Even if they were legalised you would still have to have laws to stop them from being sold to young children." *Parent*

"Legalise drugs and put a tax on them in the way that alcohol and tobacco are taxed, and use the money that's raised to pay for the treatment of people with drugs problems." *College student*

Prepare for a class debate on the motion: 'This house believes that decriminalising drugs use would do more harm than good'.

Drugs and the law

Statements on drugs	Age groups of people interviewed	
	18–34 yrs	**Over 35 yrs**
1. With regard to 'soft drugs', such as cannabis, which statement comes closest to your own view?		
The sale and possession of soft drugs should remain a criminal offence, as now	33	48
Selling or possessing soft drugs should remain illegal but should be regarded as a minor offence, such as parking in the wrong place, rather than a criminal offence	33	27
Selling or possessing soft drugs should no longer be illegal	31	19
Don't know	3	6
2. With regard to 'hard drugs', such as heroin and crack cocaine, which statement comes closest to your own view?		
The sale and possession of hard drugs should remain a criminal offence, as now	87	90
Selling or possessing hard drugs should remain illegal but should be regarded as a minor offence, such as parking in the wrong place, rather than a criminal offence	5	3
Selling or possessing hard drugs should no longer be illegal	6	5
Don't know	2	2
3. If drugs were either legalised or decriminalised, what do you think would be the effect on the number of people using drugs?		
Many more would use drugs	20	32
Some more would use them	36	35
Only a few more would use drugs	30	22
No more would use them	10	6
Don't know	4	5

TELEGRAPH YOUGOV POLL, *THE DAILY TELEGRAPH*

Study the results of the Telegraph YouGov survey above. Discuss what you learn about adults' views on changing the laws on 'soft drugs' and 'hard drugs'. How do older people's views differ from younger people's views?

FOR YOUR FILE

Imagine you are a member of a government 'think-tank' on drugs. What changes (if any) would you suggest making to the drugs laws? Give reasons for your views.

16 EMERGENCY FIRST AID

First aid: responsibilities and dealing with unconsciousness

Aim: To understand the responsibilities of a first aider and how to give emergency first aid to a casualty who is unconscious (PSHE 2h)

Being a first aider

If you were first on the scene in an emergency, would you know what to do? The best way to learn how to handle the situation is to do a first aid course. The practice you get during a course will not only help you to know what to do, but will also make you feel less apprehensive about having to cope in a real emergency.

The golden rule of first aid is that you shouldn't do anything that will cause further harm to the casualty. Prompt action may be essential in some life-threatening circumstances, but you need to know what you are doing. If you keep calm and follow the guidelines you have learned in your first aid course then there shouldn't be any repercussions. But if you panic and take inappropriate action, for example by giving treatment that causes further injury to the casualty, there could be legal consequences.

What is the golden rule of first aid? Why is it best to wait for help to arrive if you are unsure what to do?

Your responsibilities as a first aider

1 To assess a situation quickly and safely, and summon appropriate help.

2 To protect casualties and others at the scene from possible danger.

3 To identify, as far as possible, the injury or nature of the illness affecting a casualty.

4 To give each casualty early and appropriate treatment, treating the most serious conditions first.

5 To arrange for the casualty's removal to hospital, into the care of a doctor, or to his (or her) home as necessary.

6 If medical aid is needed, to remain with a casualty until further care is available.

7 To report your observations to those taking over care of the casualty, and to give further assistance if required.

8 To prevent cross-infection between yourself and the casualty as far as possible.

FROM *THE AUTHORISED MANUAL OF ST JOHN AMBULANCE, ST ANDREW'S AMBULANCE ASSOCIATION AND THE BRITISH RED CROSS*, REVISED 8TH EDITION

Discuss what your responsibilities are as a first aider. Think of ways in which these responsibilities can be achieved. Are any harder to achieve than others?

FOR YOUR FILE

Write a letter to someone who is thinking of taking a first aid course, explaining why you think it is a good idea to do so.

Dealing with unconsciousness

Knowing what to do in an emergency can save lives. Many deaths from road accidents occur from the person choking to death while lying unconscious. It is estimated that a considerable number of lives could have been saved if someone had just put the injured person in the recovery position (see right).

Unconsciousness can be caused by anything that interrupts the normal working of the brain. The most common causes of unconsciousness are heart attack, stroke, epilepsy, drug overdose, alcohol, head injury, diabetes, and poisoning.

Whatever has caused the patient to become unconscious may also have caused additional injuries. His breathing may have stopped, for example, or he may be bleeding severely. Your first priority is to deal with any of these life-threatening injuries.

Once this has been done, you can take steps to prevent the main threat to the unconscious patient: choking to death. He could choke on his own vomit or his tongue could obstruct his airway so that he cannot breathe. Putting the patient into the recovery position will eliminate these dangers.

You should NOT move any unconscious person who has had a bad fall or serious injury that may have damaged his spine. Leave him where he is until help arrives.

The recovery position

1 Before you try to turn the person, loosen any tight clothing, check that he is breathing and that his airway is clear, and remove glasses and false teeth, if present.

2 Kneel beside him on his left and tuck the hand nearest to you beneath his bottom, keeping the arm and fingers as straight as possible.

3 Cross the arm furthest from you over his chest, and the furthest leg over the nearer leg.

4 Grasp his clothing at the hip and roll him over onto your lap. Keep your right hand under his face as you turn him to protect his head.

5 Draw his top knee up so that it forms a right angle with his body, then move away from him.

6 Draw his top arm up to make a right angle with his body, and bend it at the elbow. If the ground is rough, cushion his face on this hand.

7 Make sure that his head is turned to one side, tilted well back with the chin pushed forwards.

FROM *FIRST AID* BY ELIZABETH FENWICK

The ABC of emergency first aid

When giving emergency first aid to an unconscious person, your priorities must always be **ABC**:

A is for Airway. Check that the passage between the mouth, nose, throat and windpipe is clear.

B is for Breathing. Check that the person is still breathing.

C is for Circulation. Check that the heart is still beating, and that the blood is still being circulated, by feeling for a pulse in the side of the neck.

If there are other people around, send someone for help or dial 999 yourself.

❶ **Explain what your priorities are when treating an unconscious person.**

❷ **Discuss why an unconscious person is in danger of choking and what to do to prevent this from happening.**

❸ **Practise putting each other in the recovery position.**

Treating shock and resuscitation

Aim: To examine how to treat someone for shock, and to know how to give artificial respiration to someone who has stopped breathing (PSHE 2h)

What is shock?

Shock is the term used to describe the symptoms that happen when the organs of the body – especially the brain – are deprived of blood.

What we usually think of as shock – the feeling of faintness or shakiness that can follow a slight injury or an emotional upset – is caused by a temporary loss of blood to the brain and is not life-threatening.

True medical shock occurs when there is actually less blood or body fluid available. When this happens, the body tries to keep up the blood supply to the brain at the expense of all other less important parts of the body.

What are the signs of shock?

After a severe accident, always watch for the following signs that indicate shock:

- Cold, clammy skin with heavy sweating
- Faintness, giddiness or blurring of vision
- Nausea or vomiting
- Thirst
- Confusion and anxiety
- Rapid, shallow breathing
- Rapid, feeble pulse.

Seven steps to treat shock

1 Lay the casualty down with his feet raised and his head turned to one side.

2 Deal with the cause of shock if this is possible, for instance by stopping heavy bleeding.

3 Send for help. You must get the person to hospital as soon as you can.

4 If he is unconscious or vomiting, you may need to put him in the recovery position (see page 75). But never move anyone unnecessarily, as they may have spinal or internal injuries.

5 Loosen any tight clothing.

6 Stop further heat loss. It may be possible to put a blanket under him. Cover him if he shivers, but do not use hot-water bottles or electric blankets – this only draws blood back to the skin which does not need it, and away from the vital body organs that do.

7 Do not give anything to drink (especially not alcohol).

FROM *FIRST AID* BY ELIZABETH FENWICK

FOR YOUR FILE

Write an information sheet on shock. Include what shock is, what causes it, what are the symptoms and how to treat it.

Mouth-to-mouth resuscitation

It is possible to save the life of a person who has stopped breathing by giving them mouth-to-mouth resuscitation. This provides the patient with artificial ventilation, however, you need to be trained to do this properly.

It is important to act quickly because a person who has stopped breathing is not getting any oxygen. If their brain is deprived of oxygen for more than a few minutes, they will probably suffer permanent brain damage. They need an emergency supply to their lungs to help them to start breathing again for themselves.

This is how a first aider is trained to give mouth-to-mouth resuscitation:

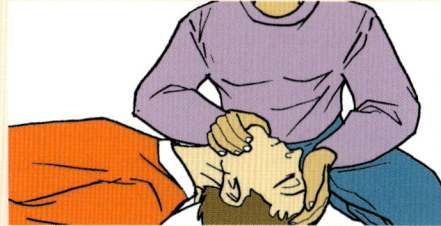

1 Lie the person on their back, tilt their head back and gently pull their lower jaw forward. Sometimes this is sufficient to start them breathing again, by bringing the tongue forward away from the airway.

2 Put a finger into their mouth to make sure that nothing, i.e. sand, seaweed or vomit, is blocking the airway.

3 Hold the mouth open and pinch the nostrils together to stop the air you breathe in coming out through their nose. If possible, use a protective device over the mouth, such as a plastic bag with a hole in it, as this is more hygienic.

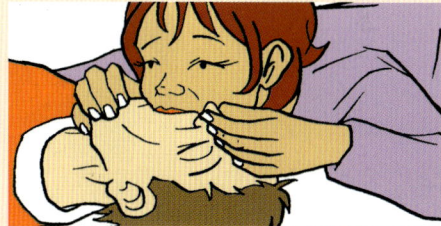

4 Take a deep breath, put your mouth over their mouth and blow into their lungs. Watch to make sure that their chest rises as the air enters their lungs, then falls when you take your mouth away. If it doesn't, then something is blocking the airway and you need to repeat stage 2.

5 Keep on breathing into the person's lungs until they start to breathe again for themselves or until medical help arrives. It may take some time for them to start breathing again, so do not give up if they don't start breathing straight away.

6 Once they start breathing again, put them in the recovery position (see page 75).

Cardio-pulmonary resuscitation (CPR)

If a casualty's heart has stopped beating, it may be possible to save their life by giving them chest compressions to keep their circulation going. These must be combined with artificial ventilation (see mouth-to-mouth resuscitation above). This combined process is known as cardio-pulmonary resuscitation, or CPR. It is essential to be trained in the use of this technique before you attempt it.

The sooner you start giving resuscitation, the more likely it is to be successful. It is also essential to call an ambulance as quickly as possible. Emergency ambulances carry a machine, called a defibrillator, which can start a person's heart beating again by applying a controlled electric shock. Paramedics can help to stabilise a casualty's condition until the person reaches hospital and receives further treatment and care.

FOR YOUR FILE

Write an information sheet on:

- **artificial ventilation – what it is, how it can save lives, and how to give it.**

- **CPR – what it stands for, and how chest compressions can keep a person alive until they receive expert medical attention.**

- **the importance of summoning an ambulance when someone needs resuscitation, and what a defibrillator is.**

17 MARRIAGE AND COMMITMENT

Attitudes to marriage and commitment

Aim: To discuss attitudes to marriage and long-term commitment, and explore their implications (PSHE 3e, 3g)

Cohabiting

The structure of families have changed in the last several decades. Instead of getting married, many people are living together or cohabiting. Some cohabiting couples eventually get married, some continue in committed unmarried relationships, and some of them break up.

Why marry?

"Marriage gives you security in your relationship."

"It's a way of making a public commitment to your partner."

"I want children and it's important to me that I am married before I have them."

"Marriage is just a legal contract. You don't need it for anything else."

"I am a Hindu. We all take marriage very seriously in our family."

"What's the point of marriage these days, unless you are religious?"

1 Discuss the different views about marriage given above. What are your own views?

2 Is cohabitation a good alternative to marriage? Is it a good way to 'test out' the relationship? What rights do people who cohabit have?

Attitudes to marriage and cohabitation

- In 1989, 70% of people thought couples should get married if they wanted children; now only 54% do.

- 67% of people think it is acceptable for a couple to cohabit, even if they don't intend to marry.

- Young people, especially young women, are unconvinced about the need for marriage: only 33% of 18–24 year olds think marriage should precede parenthood.

- However, there is still considerable support for marriage as an ideal, with only 9% dismissing it as 'just a piece of paper'. Nearly 60% of people think it is still the best kind of relationship.

- 56% incorrectly believe that unmarried people in this situation 'definitely' or 'probably' have the same rights as married people.

FROM WWW.ONEPLUSONE.ORG.UK/INFORMATION/INFO.HTM

New rights for unmarried fathers

Until December 2003, unmarried fathers had very few legal rights. Even though they may have lived with the mother of their child and played a full part in that child's upbringing, the unmarried father did not have 'parental responsibility' (PR). PR gives fathers the right to be involved in major decisions about their child, such as the right to authorise medical treatment and the right of access. Many fathers did not realise the significance of PR until the relationship with the child's mother broke down.

Under the Adoption & Children Act 2002, unmarried fathers can now obtain PR if they are registered on the birth certificate as the child's father.

They will still need the mother's consent, but this is an important development. (If the mother refuses to agree, the father can still apply for PR through the courts.)

The law now effectively recognises the father's legal position, even though he is not married to the mother.

> Discuss how the legal status of unmarried fathers has changed. What does this say about society's attitude to marriage and cohabitation? What does this say about society's attitude to the role of the father in a child's life?

Marriage and divorce: the statistics

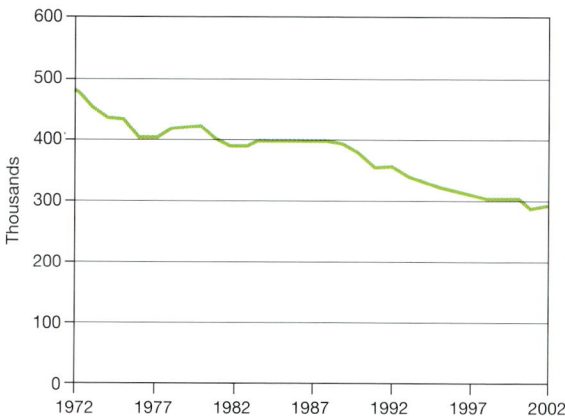

Marriages in the UK, 1972–2002

WWW.STATISTICS.GOV.UK/CCI/

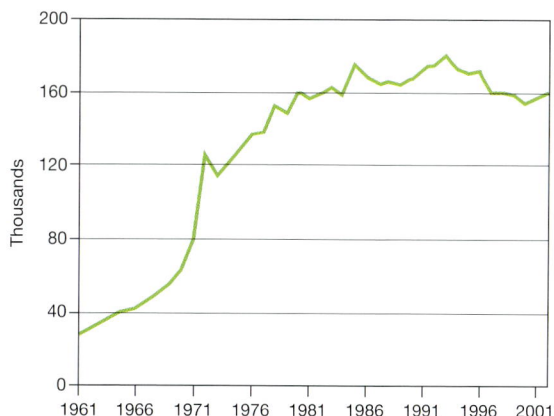

Divorces granted in the UK, 1961–2002

WWW.STATISTICS.GOV.UK/CCI/

1 There were 291 800 weddings in the UK in 2002 – that's 2% more than in 2001. How accurate is the newspaper headline: 'Weddings on the increase'?

2 The average age for first marriages in England and Wales in 2002 was 31 for men and 29 for women. In 1972 the average age was 26 for men and 23 for women. Discuss reasons why more people are marrying later in life.

In 2002, the number of divorces granted in the UK increased from 157 000 in 2001 to 160 000 in 2002. Discuss what newspaper headline you would write to deliver this news. Give a broader context in the first paragraph of your story.

The divorce rate doubled in the 1960s, then doubled again between 1969 and 1972. Research social attitudes in the 1960s and the Divorce Reform Act 1969 to find out why.

FOR YOUR FILE

"We may live in a throwaway society today: if one car doesn't suit, the fashion is to change it for another. But sadly this principle is too often applied to a partner."

Jill Curtis

Write a reply stating whether you agree or disagree. Justify your views.

Long-term relationships

Aim: To explore what it means to make a long-term relationship work (PSHE 3e, 3g)

Be a perfect partner

It's not easy; in fact, it's a lot of hard work. But it's worth the effort because the more you put into a relationship, the more you get out of it.

The key to a good relationship is mutual respect and good communication. You have to be able to talk to your partner. This means being brave enough to discuss issues that may be upsetting. If you have a problem, don't hold back. A problem that's bottled up can get out of proportion. Talking it through can ease the pressure and enable you both to find a solution.

Good communication is important for a good relationship

If your partner raises doubts about your relationship, put yourself in their shoes. Imagine how you would feel if you were them. Don't leap in and make accusations, don't get upset, let them speak – even if this means hearing things you don't like. Perhaps they have a valid point about something, which you could try and sort out.

Feeling comfortable about talking means feeling good about yourself. You need self-esteem to feel assertive. Be as true to yourself as you can. Respect your own thoughts and opinions and be honest about them. Your partner will love you for who you are. Pretending to be something you're not won't work in the long term.

Just as you should be yourself, your partner should be, too. This inevitably means that you won't agree on everything and could end up having rows. Accept that your partner has a right to their own views. You don't have to agree with those views, but you should respect them. It takes compromise to make a relationship work.

Give and take is one thing, but there may be issues on which you're not willing to compromise. It's okay not to see eye to eye on everything. It would be boring if you did. Listen to your partner's ideas and try and see it from their angle. Not finding common ground doesn't mean your relationship is doomed.

FROM ONE LIFE, BBC.CO.UK/RADIO1/ONE LIFE

❶ **Read the article 'Be a perfect partner'. Discuss what it says about making a long-term relationship work.**

❷ **Think about what is the key to a good relationship. Make a list of three key skills needed to make a relationship work and give a reason for each one.**

Arranged marriages

The wedding planners

Think you know the facts about arranged marriages?

Sanna Nasrullah sets you straight

Arranged marriages are practised mainly by Muslims, Hindus and Sikhs. The tradition began a long time ago. Parents used to get their children married off to a person of their choice because they believed that it was a sin to go out with someone before getting married.

Some parents used to organise this when their children were very young. This was not because they wanted to get rid of them but because their children started having feelings for the opposite sex at a very young age. Nowadays most parents don't try to arrange marriages until their children are at least 16 and usually much older.

Do arranged marriages work better than love marriages?

Arranged marriages often used to depend on how much money the groom earned. But that is not so important now because women are usually able to have their own careers rather than being full-time housewives.

The girl has the last word

I am a Muslim and many Muslim parents feel strongly that their children must have an arranged marriage. What people may not realise is that the girl always has the last word. (Or at least she's meant to.) If her parents pick out a boy for her, she gets to see him a few times and have dinner with him. If she does not get along with him or simply doesn't like him enough to want to marry him, then she can say 'No'. Some girls do get forced into arranged marriages but that is not what Islam teaches.

I'm going to have an arranged marriage. I trust my mum to find me the right man because no one knows me better than she does. I think people should trust their parents. I have seen in my life that arranged marriages work better than love marriages.

I believe in fate

My cousin had an arranged marriage about seven years ago. She now has three kids and is pregnant with the fourth. She is very happy with her life, and she loves her husband very much. It may help an arranged marriage to be successful if the bride and groom are strongly religious, though whatever the religion and however strong the belief it could still work. I believe that God helps arranged marriages to work, and I believe in fate.

My cousin and her husband were made for each other. Then I look at all the people who have married out of love and how those marriages didn't last. Most of my aunties and my close family have had love marriages and most of them have not worked at all. I don't know why this is, it's just the way the world works.

I'm not saying that all arranged marriages work, or that they don't. I just think people should be more open-minded to it and not just focus on the age of the girl or assume it's to do with the wealth of the husband. That kind of thing does not happen any more.

ADAPTED FROM WWW.EXPOSURE.ORG.UK/YOUTH1/MODULES

1. Discuss what you have learned about arranged marriages.

2. How would you feel if your parents or guardians wanted you to have an arranged marriage?

3. Do you agree that 'arranged marriages can work better than love marriages'? What reasons could explain this?

FOR YOUR FILE

Write a personal statement called:

'Arranged marriages: my view'.

18 PARENTHOOD AND PARENTING

Becoming a parent

Aim: To explore the effect that becoming a parent has on a person's life, particularly in relation to teenage pregnancy (PSHE 3e, 3f, 3h)

Teenage parents

Britain still tops the league of teenage pregnancies in Europe. What is the reality of being a teenage parent, and what should the government be doing to address the problem?

Big Daddy

Darren Ramsay taught baby care skills in the first *Big Brother* reality TV programme shown on *Channel 4*. He has three children, Shanice (8), Nuviea (6) and Zahnae (3)

Becoming a dad was hard because I was only 17. It was a big responsibility. I was still at college: I was going to do a business and finance course and then go into travel and tourism. Then Shanice was born and all my dreams deteriorated. It was very daunting, though I knew it would be all right.

Natalie, Shanice's mother, was 19. We'd always shared everything so we didn't want all that stuff about the woman staying at home and the man going to work. Neither of us wanted to miss out. She was studying to be a veterinary surgeon, so she gave up her dreams, too.

At first we kept up our teenage lifestyle, like going out to lunch. In the end we had to stop because it would cost £30 and we needed to get nappies and things for the baby.

When Shanice was 10 months old, Nuviea was born. Things were OK but, by the time Nuviea was six months old, things got tough. One of the babies would cry and want attention and then the other one would. One baby got a cold, then the other and soon the whole family was ill. It was harder than we expected.

Our funds were running low so I worked as a delivery driver. Natalie hated it. We had always been together, and she felt the stress of motherhood. Then the arguments started. I started work in a fashion store: no weekend work and more time with Natalie. Things got better. Crazy though it may seem, we said, "Let's have another one".

Our personal relationship got worse again during the pregnancy. I was making the bucks, she was having the baby; her hormones were going crazy and she was blaming me for everything. I'd put my key in the lock but not want to go in.

Separating took three months. That was the hardest time. I really missed my kids. I had to stop being so big-headed and stubborn, make amends and reconcile. At the end of the day, these children had two parents, whether or not they were living together.

Might we get back together? I say: "Never say never". Things are going well. We have shared so much. We are getting our lives back. Years ago, I wanted to be a presenter. I do that now. Natalie is back at college. And we have three beautiful children.

FROM *DAD* MAGAZINE

❶ **Discuss what you have learned about the experiences of Darren and Natalie from the article above.**

❷ **Make a list of the things that changed for them when they started a family. Were these changes for the better or for the worse?**

❸ **Do you think their experience would have been any different if: (a) they had waited until they were older or (b) they had been married?**

Sex education

"Young people in Britain are encouraged to regard sexual relations from an early age as desirable as long as they use contraception... The Government needs to be telling young people not to have sex yet, rather than telling them sex is fine but they need to be using contraception... Public policy should be reviewed to see if there are ways in which the traditional family, based on marriage, could be shored up rather than undermined."

Robert Whelan, Director of the Family Education Trust

Discuss the two different views held on sex education in Britain (above). Which do you think is the right approach? Which is more likely to reduce teenage pregnancy?

I want a baby

"I'll feel grown up and no one will be able to tell me what to do."
Shona

"Maybe he'll stay with me if I have his baby."
Hannah

"It's a way out. I won't have to get a job I don't like."
Teresa

"Someone will love me."
Gill

"I'll have someone cute to love."
Ruth

"I want to feel better about myself."
Jackie

"I'll get money and my own flat from the council."
Donna

FROM WWW.THESTRAIGHTTALKINGPROJECT.CO.UK/WHY.HTML

❶ **Look at the reasons above given by teenage girls who want a baby. Discuss each reason in turn and decide whether you think it is a good reason for having a baby.**

❷ **Imagine a friend gives you one of the reasons above for trying for a baby. Write notes on your reply and be prepared to share them with the class.**

Deciding whether to start a family is one of the most important decisions a couple has to make.

❶ **Make a list of all the positive aspects of starting a family. Include all the pleasures that parenthood brings.**

❷ **Make a list of all the reasons why you may not want to start a family. What responsibilities and problems does parenthood bring?**

❸ **As a class, discuss whether your assessment would change depending on circumstances, such as your age when starting a family.**

Parenthood

Aim: To explore the roles and responsibilities of parents (PSHE 3e, 3f, 3h)

Being a parent

Being a parent will probably be the most rewarding thing you'll ever do, and the toughest. This is because there are certain responsibilities that come with being a parent, and there are certain things that children need and that parents need to do.

Some of the qualities you need as a parent remain important all through your children's lives – above all, showing love and giving physical care. However, you will have to show these qualities in different ways as your children grow up.

Different generations – children need parents to show different qualities as they grow up

NEW BABY

What your baby needs

Everything – a new baby is totally dependent on you to get what they need.

Patience and understanding – she can only tell you she is unhappy by crying and it takes time to work out what she wants.

Lots of attention – by responding to her cries and showing that you care when she's distressed, your baby will learn that she is loved.

What you need

Time for you, and your partner if you have one, to adjust to the changes a new baby brings.

Patience and understanding – the demands of a newborn can be emotionally and physically exhausting, especially during the first few weeks. As well as having no time to yourself, relationships can come under strain.

To look after yourself, as well as your baby – accept help from friends, family, neighbours.

TODDLERS

What your toddler needs

To be able to **develop her personality**.

To learn about the world and discover what she can and what she can't do – this might seem like she is testing you all the time.

To be allowed to do as much as possible for herself.

To be encouraged and praised for any good behaviour, e.g. sharing.

To have set limits on behaviour, e.g. "Hitting hurts. Say it with words."

What you need

Time to recharge your batteries – this can be an exhausting and challenging time

To spend time with your partner, if you have one. If you are on your own, try to find ways you can spend some time with grown-ups, so that you get some breaks from your child, e.g. join a parent and toddler group.

FROM PARENTLINE PLUS

How to be... a 'good enough' parent

Forget trying to be the perfect parent – it's impossible. Try to be 'good enough', which means you'll need to show:

- **love, love, love** – a bottomless supply, especially in the first few years when you are building up your child's self-esteem. Love also means providing physical care – warmth, rest and nutritious meals.

- **self-sacrifice** – children need a huge amount of time and attention. This will mean making sacrifices, especially when they are very young.

- **consistency** – children like routines, and need to know what the ground rules are for behaviour. Consistent but not over-strict rules help them feel secure and allow you to manage behavioural problems.

- **listening skills** – always listen to what your children have to say. They deserve your attention and respect, and will grow in confidence if they are listened to.

- **a sense of humour** – especially at 4am when your four-year-old son wants to dress up as Batman for his party at midday, or when your teenage daughter phones late at night to ask for a lift home.

1 **Discuss what you have learned about being a parent. What skills and qualities do parents need to have in order to care for (a) a new baby and (b) a toddler?**

2 **Make a list of what children need:**
   (a) from ages 4 to 11
   (b) at adolescence (12+).

FOR YOUR FILE

Write a paragraph explaining why you should aim to be 'a good enough parent' rather than 'a perfect parent'.

What is a mother?

She's the one we turn to
when we feel lost and sad,
she's our steadying anchor,
the best friend we've ever had.

She's the one who went without
to keep us clothed and fed,
the one who dried our tears,
and tucked us up in bed.

She's the one who understood
our childhood hopes and fears,
the one who praised our efforts
through all our growing years.

FROM *SMELLS OF CHILDHOOD*
BY MARY M DONOGHUE

What is a father?

"There is a difference between a father and a dad. A dad comes every now and then to give the mother money if the child needs anything. A father is there for his child whenever. He speaks to his child, advises his child, makes the child see the world. I see myself as a father, because my dad was a dad."
Richard, 19

FROM BABYFATHERS: *NEW IMAGES OF TEENAGE FATHERHOOD*
BY EDMUND CLARK

Read 'What is a father?' and 'What is a mother?' and discuss these questions:

1 **Does Mary Donoghue give a realistic picture of what a mother is? Could you be this kind of mother? What does the poem leave out?**

2 **What was Richard's experience of his own father? Explain what kind of father he wants to be. Has he left anything out?**

19 CHALLENGING OFFENSIVE BEHAVIOUR

Sexism and sexual harassment

Aim: To examine what sexism and sexual harassment are, and to explore how to challenge them
(PSHE 3a, 3c/Citizenship 1a, 2a, 2b, 2c)

What is sexism?

Sexism is when we treat a person differently, purely because they are of a particular sex. Imagine a man and a woman both applying for the same job. Both people have similar backgrounds and qualifications. An employer may want to employ the man, because the office is full of men and he feels the man would fit in better. However, this is illegal, because it is sexual discrimination – treating someone differently because of his or her sex.

① **Look at these examples of sexism that you may have encountered. What other examples can you think of?**

"Girls are brighter than boys."

"Girls are better at languages, but boys are better at science."

"Boys are better than girls at sport."

"It's more important for a boy to have a career than a girl."

② **Make a list of attitudes that you think are sexist. Compare your lists in a class discussion.**

Why is sexism damaging?

Sexism is present in our society in many ways. Examples of sexism towards women are that women are often paid less than men who have the same job, and often receive less responsibility. In the UK, the term 'glass ceiling' is used, describing how a woman can progress to a certain level within a company, but no further.

Sexism is damaging because it doesn't allow people to fulfil their potential. In the case of sexism towards women, it can hold women back, deny them opportunities, and make it harder for them to assert their independence.

"Women are often judged by their appearance rather than their ability to do a job."

"Even today, there are still some jobs that most people regard as 'men's jobs' and other jobs that people regard as 'women's jobs'."

"Why it is that when a man is looking after the children at home people look down on him?"

"We need stronger laws when it comes to sexual discrimination. And women should stand up for themselves – whenever you find sexual discrimination, report it!"

Discuss the statements (left). Which do you agree with? Give reasons for your views.

Short skirts ruled 'sexist'

An executive who claimed she was sacked for refusing to wear short skirts has been awarded £18 000 compensation.

Hilary Paterson, a 30-year-old recruitment consultant, told a tribunal in Edinburgh that her boss judged her on physical appearance rather than her ability to do the job. The tribunal ruled yesterday that his remarks amounted to sexual discrimination.

FROM THE DAILY TELEGRAPH

Sexual harassment

Sexual harassment is another form of sexism. This is when a person repeatedly pesters or is a nuisance towards another person, through their behaviour. This behaviour could include making sexual advances. Although sometimes the behaviour may appear to be 'innocent', to the person that the harassment is directed at it can be uncomfortable, off-putting, and even threatening.

Discuss the examples of behaviour on the right. Which do you think qualify as sexual harassment? Why?

> Wolf whistling

> Putting your arm around someone

> Saying somebody looks nice, once

> Asking somebody out once

> Saying somebody looks nice, repeatedly

> Refusing to take 'No' for an answer when someone doesn't want to go out with you

Case study: street harassment

Shouting at girls, is, in fact, an act of hostility. No one shouts sexual remarks at someone he or she loves or respects. Men and boys who do shout at women do it because they think treating women as objects is 'cool', and that it gives them the upper hand.

Sometimes a man will harass a woman as an expression of his own insecurity – dislike for himself, perhaps, and an inability to believe that any female could really like him. Other times the hostility is based on race or class. Some workmen, for example, seem to enjoy harassing women dressed in office clothing. The hostility can be disguised as flattery, but often it's right out there in the open.

Shouting at women is an example of street harassment

FROM *STAND UP FOR YOURSELF* BY HELEN BENEDICT

① **Discuss what you have learned about street harassment. Why do you think some men shout sexual remarks at women?**

② **Think about the situation of a group of women out drinking on a Friday night. Are there ever situations when women behave in a similar way to men?**

FOR YOUR FILE

Design a poster as part of a campaign against sexual harassment. Think about the key messages you would like to get across.

Challenging sexism

Erica Stewart suggests ways to get rid of sexism in society

If you want to get rid of sexism in society, it's not only important to recognise it but to challenge it. To do so, you need to know what the law is – what the Sex Discrimination Act says – and to be assertive.

It helps if you have other people who are willing to support your challenge, so, for example, if it is a case of sexism in the work place, you may be able to get a Trade Union representative involved. Whatever you do, don't ignore it. Otherwise it will continue.

Sexism in the work place can be quite common. Discuss what action you should take in each of the situations below.

> **One of your work colleagues, a boy with long hair, is told by the boss to get it cut, because he "looks like a girl".**

> **A group of young men put a photo of a topless model up in a staffroom and joke about it in front of the women who share the staffroom.**

> **You are a married woman, and during a job interview one of the interviewers asks you whether or not you have children, or are planning to have them.**

Homosexuality and homophobia

Aim: To understand what homosexuality and homophobia are, and the different attitudes towards homosexuality that exist (PSHE 3a, 3c/Citizenship 1a, 2a, 2b, 2c)

What is homosexuality?

Homosexuality is when a person is attracted to members of the same sex. Men who are attracted to other men are called 'gay'. Women who are attracted to women are known as 'lesbians'. Sometimes, a person's sexual orientation may be attraction towards members of both sexes. These people are known as 'bisexuals'.

The majority of people in the UK are heterosexual – they are attracted to people of the opposite sex. As a result, many myths have grown up about homosexuals. Here are some of them:

Homosexual couples are often discriminated against

> **"You can tell homosexuals from their appearance and behaviour."**

MYTH: Some people think that all gay men are 'effeminate' and that all lesbians are 'butch'. The fact is that there is as much variety in the appearance and behaviour of homosexuals as there is between heterosexuals.

> **"Homosexuals dislike people of the opposite sex."**

MYTH: Homosexuals may like and dislike people of either sex, just like heterosexuals do.

> **"Homosexuals fancy everyone who is of the same sex as them."**

MYTH: Just because you like someone of one sex, doesn't mean you like everyone of that sex. It's the same for homosexuals.

How society discriminates against homosexuals

A fear of homosexuals is known as 'homophobia'. This can lead to prejudice and harassment – where people treat homosexuals badly purely because of who they are attracted to. In the UK such behaviour is against the law. For example, you can't turn down a person for a job just because of their sexual orientation.

'Hate crimes' are when people attack homosexuals purely because they are homosexual. However hate crimes are not just directed at people who are homosexual. The law imposes heavier penalties in recognition of this type of crime.

There are also more subtle forms of discrimination that occur every day against homosexuals in the UK. Because most people are heterosexual, the rules that govern our society have grown up to promote heterosexuality and discriminate against homosexuality. Homosexual couples are discriminated against because they cannot marry and have the same rights as married couples.

The UK Government is currently changing the law in the way that it treats homosexuals. In the future, homosexuals will be able to enter into a legally binding agreement, which will allow them to be treated as if they were married. Thus, homosexual couples that have made a long-term commitment to each other will be able to leave an inheritance to their partner should they die, and for it to be taxed in exactly the same way as if they were married.

❶ **Discuss the myths about homosexuality (above). Can you think of any other myths?**

❷ **Why do you think these myths might be damaging?**

Discuss how homosexuals are discriminated against in the UK. Make a list of key points to discuss with the class.

Different attitudes towards homosexuality

In the UK, there are different attitudes towards homosexuals and homosexuality. For instance, the Catholic Church disapproves of the act of two people of the same sex making love. Some Methodist Christians believe that a permanent relationship that includes love is an appropriate way of expressing sexuality, whatever the sexes of the two partners in the relationship.

Homosexual groups, such as Stonewall, believe that hatred of homosexuals is a social evil, equal to racism and sexism. Stonewall argues there should be equal treatment for all men and women, whatever their sexual orientation.

Look at the statements (right). Which do you agree with? Give reasons for your views.

> "I can understand homosexuals being attracted to one another. But they shouldn't be allowed to get married – that's a Christian idea and should be kept for people of the same sex."

> "Homosexuals should be entitled to exactly the same rights as heterosexuals, and be treated in exactly the same way."

> "I'm all for homosexual rights. But some gay people shouldn't ram the fact that they are gay down other people's throats. In order to be treated equally, they should act exactly like other people and not make a big thing of it."

Why is homophobia damaging?

Preconditioned by things such as TV and advertising, it's assumed that every boy and girl is straight (heterosexual)...

There is tremendous pressure on us all to conform, to become objects of desire to the opposite sex, to get married and to have children...

The problem is intensified by the fact that in our culture there still exists a taboo against homosexuality. This taboo exists mainly because there is an old idea that 'sex equals reproduction' and as loving someone of the same sex can't produce babies, many see it as 'unnatural', 'abnormal', or even 'perverted'.

Insulting words such as 'poofter', 'faggot', 'queer', 'bender' and 'dyke' have been invented to reinforce this prejudice and they cause a lot of harm. These prejudices make many homosexual people feel that if they are attracted to the same sex there must be something wrong with them and they end up feeling bad about themselves and their sexuality.

FROM *HOMOSEXUALITY* BY ROSALYN CHISSICK

What is homophobia? Where do you think homophobia comes from? Why do you think it is damaging?

Discuss the situations below and what you should do in each case to challenge homophobia.

> One of your friends is getting bullied by a group of other teenagers, because they have discovered that he is gay.

> You hear a hotel owner refusing to give two men a double room, because he says "it's a family hotel".

> You see someone spraying homophobic graffiti outside a flat where a lesbian couple live.

FOR YOUR FILE

Someone you know is being bullied because she is a lesbian. Write about how you would deal with this situation if it happened
(a) at school, and
(b) outside school.

20 CO-OPERATING ON A COMMUNITY PROJECT

Volunteering

Aim: To examine what volunteering involves and how it can benefit you and your local community (Citizenship 1f, 2a, 2b, 2c, 3b, 3c)

What is volunteering?

A volunteer is someone who does a task or job for free. Volunteering can be done over any period of time, anywhere. Some people may volunteer to pick litter up in their local park for an afternoon. Others may volunteer to help out at their local day centre for older people once a week for a month. Some people may choose to help out in their local charity shop every Saturday during a gap year.

People volunteer for many different reasons. Usually they want to contribute something to their local community. However, there are also several ways that the person can benefit from volunteering. These include:

- developing transferable skills that can be used in other jobs
- filling up free time
- receiving training that will help them in their career
- gaining practical on-the-job experience
- pursuing a particular form of work they enjoy
- getting job satisfaction from a task well done.

Do you know anyone that has done any voluntary work? What do you think their reasons for doing voluntary work were? Why might you want to do voluntary work in the future?

Look at the three examples below. What sort of organisation have these people been volunteering for? What do you think they got out of it? Write down your answers.

> "I did some voluntary work running a youth workshop which helped young people learn how to budget and save money. It was very rewarding and helped me refresh my own budgeting skills."

> "I helped clean up a riverbank for the local council. I learned a lot about how it is important to recycle, and what damage certain types of rubbish can do. I now have several weeks experience that I can show to an employer, and my team leader gave me a reference."

> "I got involved building a skate park. It was fun helping design the park, and I learned a lot about working with other people."

Get involved – what young people said

A recent survey showed that young people said they would be willing to give up at least one day of their time for a good cause.

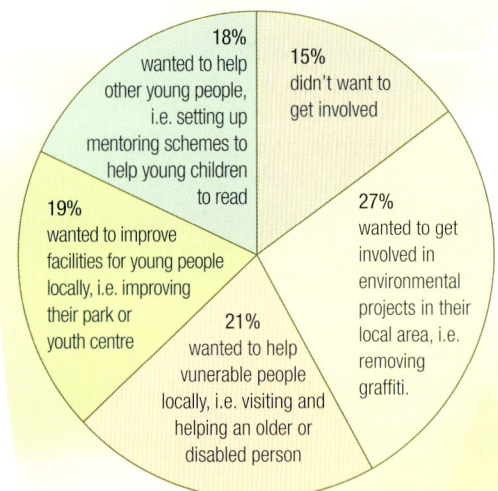

- 18% wanted to help other young people, i.e. setting up mentoring schemes to help young children to read
- 15% didn't want to get involved
- 19% wanted to improve facilities for young people locally, i.e. improving their park or youth centre
- 27% wanted to get involved in environmental projects in their local area, i.e. removing graffiti.
- 21% wanted to help vunerable people locally, i.e. visiting and helping an older or disabled person

Case study: Community Service Volunteers

Community Service Volunteers (CSV) is a charity that seeks to involve people in short- or long-term voluntary projects. Each year, CSV finds over 100 000 volunteers something interesting to do. As a result, CSV run a number of different schemes to help people get involved with voluntary work in their local community. Two of these schemes are MADD and Millennium Volunteers.

Volunteering can help improve your environment

Make a Difference Day

Make a Difference Day (MADD) is held on the last Saturday of October each year. The idea is to give people the chance to try volunteering in their local area for just a day or an afternoon. In 2003, CSV managed to get around 50 000 people involved. Most of these had not tried volunteering before. Often, this meant that people could try volunteering again.

The idea of MADD is that it gives people a chance to do something very different. For example, this could include cutting hedges, giving blood, renovating a community centre, or reading with children for an afternoon. In 2005, MADD hopes to organise over 3000 events around the UK.

Millennium Volunteers

Millennium Volunteers is a series of projects organised by the Government. There are 130 millennium volunteer projects across England. 27 of these are run in partnership with CSV.

The aim of Millennium Volunteers is to get people between the ages of 16–24 involved in projects that are interesting to young people. The volunteering is medium- to long-term – volunteers receive a special certificate for completing 100 hours voluntary work, and an 'Award of Excellence' for completing 200 hours of voluntary work.

So far, around 100 000 people are involved in different projects around the UK. These have included:

- a community arts project to remove graffiti from an area and provide alternative forms of art for young people to create for their community
- a local enterprise project to build an adventure playground for young people on a piece of industrial wasteland
- a crime awareness project helping redesign a housing estate to make it safer for local people.

Imagine you had to get involved in either MADD or Millennium Volunteers. Which scheme would you choose to get involved with? Why? How would you hope to benefit from each scheme?

Meeting the needs of the community

Volunteering isn't about just getting something for you. It's also about meeting the needs of the community. Sometimes it will be apparent how these needs match up. For example, you may want to become a teacher and a local nursery needs volunteers to help young children with their reading skills. By helping out, you help the nursery and your teaching career.

FOR YOUR FILE

Find out about local volunteering schemes in your area. What opportunities do you think could be expanded upon to create more voluntary roles in the future?

Getting involved in a community project

Aim: To explore how to choose, get involved and complete a community volunteer project (Citizenship 1f, 2a, 2b, 2c, 3b, 3c)

Meeting the needs of the local community

Most volunteer projects are undertaken in order to directly benefit the local community in some way. A successful voluntary project:

- meets the needs of the local community
- meets the needs of the volunteers
- is carefully managed so that both needs are realistic and achievable.

There are two ways of identifying what community issues would benefit from a voluntary project. One is to simply walk round and see what needs doing in your local area. Is there much graffiti? Are there enough facilities for young people?

A second approach is to conduct a survey of people to find out what they think needs doing. This will give you a clear idea of what local people think the priorities are for their area. This is important – if you pick an issue that people think is a priority, you'll get more volunteers to help you with your project.

Resources needed

The following resources are needed to make a voluntary project work:

1. Human resources

- Volunteers, and sometimes specialist help. Find volunteers through holding meetings or placing an advert. Local media, such as the local newspaper or radio station, may be willing to help for free.

2. Financial resources

- Enough money to fund the project. This could be donated, for example, through sponsorship by a local business, or money available from a charity, the local council, or the government.

3. Raw materials

- These may be available from the school, a local business, or a local charity.

Getting involved

These are some of the voluntary projects carried out by schools throughout the UK.

Developing a mentor project, where older pupils help younger ones with a variety of issues, whether it's tackling bullying at school, developing reading skills, or staying healthy.

Setting aside an area of the school to be used as an environment centre, either by planting flowers or creating a pond, to increase the biodiversity, or number of different living creatures at the school.

Starting an after-school keep-fit club to encourage students to eat healthily, exercise regularly, and be aware of health issues, like the dangers of smoking.

Developing a community arts project, where everyone can use school arts facilities after school, to brighten up the local area, prevent graffiti spraying, and encourage young people to be involved in art.

Developing an after-school work club to maximise work experience opportunities locally and train young people, through a partnership between local businesses and students.

Look at the list of voluntary projects above. Which do you think would be the most important to your area? Why? Give reasons for your views.

Choose one of the voluntary projects from the list above. What resources will you need to make sure this project will be successful? Compare your ideas with other groups.

Planning a voluntary project

Once you have decided what resources you need, you then need to plan your project in detail. This involves:

- breaking down your project into manageable stages
- developing a clear timetable
- deciding how you will measure the success of your project.

Case study: organising an environmental awareness day

Marcy decides to organise an environmental awareness day to encourage more people to recycle in her town. Having held a meeting, she has four volunteers that will help her. Together they decide to organise a stall in the centre of town in order to get 50 new households to start some form of recycling.

Manageable stages

Marcy decides to break the project down into manageable stages and gives a role to each of her volunteers:

1. Emma is to talk to the local council about what help they can offer to people to encourage recycling, such as the location of any recycling bins, and whether the council runs any recycling box schemes.
2. Jo is to design posters about the event and materials to hand out at the stall.
3. Rafiq is to keep track of who is coming, at what time, and how long they can help at the stall for.
4. Jake is put in charge of dealing with the media, including writing letters to the paper and giving a radio interview.
5. Marcy's role is that of project manager. She will be checking everyone else is doing his or her job, and covering in case anyone is ill or too busy.

Developing a clear timetable

As project manager, Marcy develops, and is in charge of, a timetable for the project.

Week 1: Emma will approach the council.

Week 2: Jo will have finished the posters by the end of the week and everyone will help distribute them. Jake will have also written to the local paper.

Week 3: Marcy will check with Rafiq how many people are coming, and decide what areas they think they can cover.

Week 4: Marcy and Rafiq check the final numbers of attendees. She will also check that the project is still achievable, and will do a radio interview with Jake.

Measuring the success of the project

The final stage of any project is to measure if you have achieved your goal. One way of finding out is to conduct another survey, of either the people involved in the project, and/or members of the general public, to get feedback on what went right and what went wrong. Did the members of the general public feel that the project made a difference? Sometimes this may throw up new problems that need to be solved – in which case you have a new project for the next group of volunteers!

Look at one particular project from the list on page 92 or choose your own. What will be the aim of your project? How will you decide whether it has been a success or not? How will you break your project down into manageable stages?

21 REVIEWING AND RECORDING YOUR LEARNING

What you have learned

Aim: To review and record what you have learned from studying the units in *Your Life 5*

How to use this section

- Think about what you have learned in each of the four sections of the course.
- Use the questions below on each section to draft a statement about the knowledge and skills you have developed from studying the units in that section.
- In your statements include any important views, expressing your attitudes and values that you have formed as a result of considering and discussing particular topics.

Here's what Corine wrote as part of her statement about what she had learned from the unit on marriage and commitment in the Developing relationships section.

It made me realise that just because you're attracted to someone and are in love with them, there are lots of other things to consider before you commit yourself to getting married. I learned a lot about relationships and how to make them work, for example, how important it is to communicate with your partner, especially to say what you really think and feel about difficult issues. It also taught me that you need to think about how you'd both deal with any changes that arise during your marriage, like becoming parents.

Section 1: Developing as a citizen

Use these questions to help you to draft a statement about what you learned from this section.

What did you learn...

... about the UK and its relations with the rest of the world? (Citizenship 1i, 2a, 2b, 2c, pages 6–13)
- about issues concerning the UK's relationship with the EU
- about the organisation and aims of the Commonwealth and the United Nations.

... about human rights issues? (Citizenship 1a, 2a, 2b, 2c, pages 14–17)
- about cases of abuse of human rights, and about how human rights can be protected and enforced.

... about media matters? (Citizenship 1g, 2a, 2b, 2c, pages 18–23)
- about the importance of a free press
- about the media's role in society and how it provides information and affects opinion.

... about business and finance? (Citizenship 1e, 2a, 2b, 2c, pages 24–27)
- about how the UK economy works, including the role of small businesses
- about how the government manages the economy.

... about the global economy? (Citizenship 1e, 2a, 2b, 2c, pages 28–31)
- about the effects of globalisation and the issue of free trade versus fair trade
- about Third World debt, how it was created and the problems it causes.

... about global challenges? (Citizenship 1j, 2a, 2b, 2c, pages 32–35)
- about the arms trade, weapons of mass destruction and terrorism.

... about environmental issues? (Citizenship 1j, 2a, 2b, 2c, pages 36–39)
- about the environmental problems facing the world
- about sustainable development
- about action being taken both globally and locally, through Local Agenda 21.

... about working for change? (Citizenship 1f, 2a, 2b, 2c, 3b, 3c, pages 40–43)
- about international pressure groups, how they operate and about how you can get involved.

Section 2: Understanding yourself

What have you learned from this section? Use these questions to help you to draft a statement.

What did you learn...

... about developing your own values?
(PSHE 1b/Citizenship 2a, 2b, 2c, pages 44–47)

- about yourself, your opinions and your values by discussing moral and social issues, such as human cloning.

... about managing your time and studies?
(PSHE 1a, pages 48–51)

- about how to revise effectively
- about strategies to use when preparing for and taking examinations in order to reduce exam stress.

... about thinking ahead: planning your future?
(PSHE 1f, 1g, pages 52–57)

- about the career and educational opportunities open to you
- about what personal qualities you have and which career paths might be suitable for you.

... about managing your money? (PSHE 1e, pages 58–61)

- about ways you can borrow money and buy on credit
- about how to avoid getting into debt
- about the financial aspects of starting work.

Section 3: Keeping healthy

Use these questions to help you to draft a statement about what you learned from this section.

What did you learn...

... about managing stress and dealing with depression? (PSHE 2c, pages 62–65)

- About the causes, symptoms and treatments for stress and depression
- about ways of dealing with stress and depression.

... about safer sex? (PSHE 2a, 2b, 2e, 2f, 3b, pages 66–69)

- the risks involved in sexual activity
- about the various types of sexually transmitted infections, including HIV/AIDS
- about how to protect yourself from catching an STI
- about attitudes to HIV/AIDS.

... drugs and drugtaking? (PSHE 2a, 2b, 2e, pages 70–73)

- about why young people take drugs
- about the risks of drugtaking
- about the current laws concerning illegal drugs and the arguments for and against changing them.

... about emergency first aid? (PSHE 2h, pages 74–77)

- about your responsibilities as a first aider
- about how to recognise and deal with someone suffering from shock
- about the basic first aid procedures for dealing with an unconscious person
- about the techniques that first aiders use to resuscitate someone.

Section 4: Developing relationships

What did you learn from this section? Use these questions to help you to draft a statement.

What did you learn...

... about marriage and commitment? (PSHE 3e, 3g, pages 78–81)

- about attitudes to marriage and cohabitation
- about what marriage means and why people marry
- about what you need to think about before making a long-term commitment in order to make a relationship work.

... about parenthood and parenting? (PSHE 3h, pages 82–85)

- about the effect becoming a parent has on a person's life
- about the roles and responsibilities of parents
- about what children need and the qualities of good parenting.

... about challenging offensive behaviour? (PSHE 3a, 3c/Citizenship 1a, 2a, 2b, 2c, pages 86–89)

- about sexism and sexual harassment, and their effects
- about homosexuality, homophobia and discrimination against homosexuals.

... about co-operating on a community project? (Citizenship 1f, 2a, 2b, 2c, 3b, 3c, pages 90–93)

- about volunteering, how it can be of benefit to you as well as to the community, and about the opportunities that exist for voluntary work
- about how to work co-operatively and to participate in a project that is of benefit to the local community.

INDEX